Leader

MW00473945

Polished

"Tiffany has captured the most critical elements of today's professional development and authentic leadership viewed through a business etiquette lens—all while providing a contemporary refreshment of timeless key pearls. The reader will experience immediate benefit from this guidance by putting into practice this learning and easy application. This is an essential resource that will pay long-term dividends on several levels for the reader's career conquest."

—**Richard Davis,** CEO of Make-a-Wish® America
(formerly Chairman and CEO of US Bancorp)

"In a time dominated by abbreviated text messaging, two-dimensional conversation, and hybrid work, etiquette is probably the last thing on people's minds, and it should not be. First impressions remain a critical part of driving business and personal outcomes, and the principles of etiquette are as important today as they have ever been. Tiffany Adams uses her years of experience in instructing corporate teams and brings these principles to life in fun and practical ways that help the reader absorb important tools and strategies in an easily digestible manner."

—**Leigh Fox,** CEO and President, altafiber
(formerly known as Cincinnati Bell)

"*Polished* is a masterpiece. This book invited me on an incredible journey of self-reflection, analyzing critical attributes of human behavior, defining those attributes with colorful characters and fun vignettes, all while equipping me with clear and concise actions on how to be better. It's an essential read for any professional with the ambition to advance, and, frankly, any person who ever interacts with another human being. I will never give this book away because it's a reference guide for life. It's like one of those trusty textbooks that taught something important, and you keep returning to it for more guidance in the modern workplace."

—**Lee Henderson,** Partner, Ernst & Young LLP

"*Polished* is a jam-packed toolbox for business professionals at all career stages, presented in an enjoyable mix of formats that will keep you engaged and thinking. After you read it once, leave it on your desk with a notepad because there will be something every day of your business life to make you take out one of those tools and put it to work."

—**Bill Nolan,** Columbus Managing Partner,
Barnes & Thornburg LLP and Harvard Law School JD

"At a time when organizations are challenged to sustain positive and professional work cultures because of the brutality resulting from the pandemic, Tiffany Adams has created an essential read by detailing specific approaches that affect positive cultural change. It's useless when leaders have the knowledge and experience but can't engage with others. This book is a critical reminder that, in an increasingly remote and diverse workplace, relationships are vital and these strategies are timeless. Business books can be informational; however, *Polished* provides thoughtful takeaways for a compelling path forward to success and inclusivity. Each chapter emboldens the reader to celebrate personal strengths. Invest in yourself and grab a copy today."

—**Jay Rammes,** Managing Director and CPA,
Barnes Dennig & Co. Ltd.

"*Polished* is a must-read for everyone at all stages of professional life. Lessons on leadership and etiquette are illustrated through entertaining vignettes allowing the reader to learn through the blunders (and successes) of others, which is a much better alternative than learning through one's own mistakes. Read this book and get ready to be your best professional self."

—**Lee M. Stautberg,** Esq., Partner, Dinsmore & Shohl LLP

Polished

THE GUIDE TO EXCELLENCE FOR THE MODERN PROFESSIONAL

Tiffany L. Adams

RIVER GROVE
BOOKS

Published by River Grove Books,
an imprint of Greenleaf Book Group
Austin, TX
www.rivergrovebooks.com

Distributed by River Grove Books

Design and composition by Greenleaf Book Group and Kimberly Lance
Cover design by Greenleaf Book Group and Kimberly Lance
Cover image ©GettyImages/jroballo

Publisher's Cataloging-in-Publication data is available.

Print ISBN: 978-1-63299-582-7

eBook ISBN: 978-1-63299-583-4

First Edition

Dedication

To the wind beneath my wings, my mom

To the love of my life, my husband

* FOR THE AUTHOR'S MESSAGES TO THESE LOVED ONES AND OTHERS, SEE THE LETTERS OF DEDICATION AND ACKNOWLEDGMENT AT THE BACK.

"We are what we repeatedly do.
Excellence, then, is not an act but a habit."

— ARISTOTLE

Contents

INTRODUCTION   1

What Does Business Etiquette Have to Do with Leadership? Everything.

How to Read This Book   3

BUILDING BLOCK 1   5

Principles of Professionalism (POP!)

Week 1: The Power of Self-Awareness Part 1   7
—Project More Confidence

Week 2: The Power of Self-Awareness Part 2   15
—Project More Credibility

Week 3: The Power of Self-Restraint Part 1   17
—Earn Trust in Leadership

Week 4: The Power of Self-Restraint Part 2   26
—Exude a Powerful You

BUILDING BLOCK 2   29

Favorable First Impressions

Week 1: Elevate Your Likeability   31

Week 2: Discard Distracting Verbal Fillers: 38
Uh, Like, Kinda, Ya Know

Week 3: Handshake Fails and Flops   42

Week 4: Distinguished Dining in the Professional World   47

BUILDING BLOCK 3   53

The Art of Meaningful Relationship-Building

Week 1: The Power of Empathy Part 1   55

Week 2: The Power of Empathy Part 2   64

Week 3: The Power of Building Relationship Capital   67

Week 4: Grow Your Network   74

BUILDING BLOCK 4 — 77

Brilliant Conversation and Keen Listening

Week 1: Turning Difficult Conversations into Civil Discourse   79

Week 2: Curiosity—Your Gateway to Engagement   86

Week 3: Keen Listening—The North Star of a Great Leader   95

Week 4: Captivating Conversation Starters   103

BUILDING BLOCK 5 — 107

Working a Room with a Plan and Networking for Results

Week 1: Steer Clear of 5 Networking Blunders   109

Week 2: Pre-Event, At the Event, and Post-Event Strategies   122

Week 3: The Forgotten Network—Dormant Relationships   131

Week 4: Download a Networking App   136

BUILDING BLOCK 6 — 137

Executive Presence and Authentic Leadership

Week 1: What Executive Presence Is Not   139

Week 2: Executive Presence and Why Leaders Need It   143

Week 3: Ignite a Growth Mindset with 2 Power Traits   149

Week 4: Avoid the Pitfalls of Inauthentic Leadership   157

BUILDING BLOCK 7 — 163

Virtual Communication and the Inclusive Remote Workplace

Week 1: New Greeting Etiquette Emerges in a Touchless Society   165

Week 2: Mitigate Virtual Fatigue and Maximize Productivity   169

Week 3: Screen Likeability and Leading Remote Teams with 8 Best Practices   181

Week 4: Be Your Finest Virtual Communicator   195

BUILDING BLOCK 8   **201**

Catalyzing Your Personal Brand

Week 1: Identify Your Unique Value Proposition   203

Week 2: Marketing Your Business for One   213

Week 3: Define Your Target Audience   219

Week 4: Your Time to Shine   222

BUILDING BLOCK 9   **223**

Words Matter: Speak with Authority and Power Body Language

Week 1: Verbal Taboos and Weak Speak to Avoid   225

Week 2: Polished Prose: Punctuation and Grammar Matter   234

Week 3: Power Body Language and   238
Self-Calming Gestures to Avoid

Week 4: Test Your Nonverbal Communication   245

BUILDING BLOCK 10   **249**

Proper Netiquette—Email Etiquette

Week 1: Steer Clear of Email Blunders   251

Week 2: Excellent Emails—Be Brief. Be Brilliant. Be Gone.   254

Week 3: The 5 Cs of Excellent Emails   265

Week 4: Closing Salutations to Impress   267

BUILDING BLOCK 11   **269**

Proper "Netiquette"—LinkedIn and Smartphone Etiquette

Week 1: LinkedIn   271
—Avoid 3 Blunders to Boost Your Online Brand

Week 2: LinkedIn   274
—Post with Purpose and Power

Week 3: Smartphone Etiquette Rings True   281

Week 4: Navigate LinkedIn for Results   285

BUILDING BLOCK 12   **287**

The Art of Remote and In-Person Negotiations

Week 1: The Skill of Powerful Persuasion   289

Week 2: Discover This About Your Counterpart   291

Week 3: The 8-Part Framework to Win-Win Negotiations   296

Week 4: Tactics for Remote Negotiations   310

The Capstone: Culmination of the 12 Building Blocks and Your Next Steps   315

Capstone Book Quiz: How Polished Are You?   323

Conclusion and Encouragement to the Reader   329

Letters of Dedication   331

Letters of Acknowledgment   336

A Note of Gratitude from the Author   345

About the Author   347

What Does Business Etiquette Have to Do with Leadership? Everything.

How does a leader inspire a team who doesn't feel respected? It's impossible. Most leaders focus their attention on strategic direction and bottom-line results because they must answer to clients, shareholders, bosses, and boards. As a result, they often miss the quiet signs of how their relationships with their employees are evolving and don't glean a true sense of the impact of their behavior, words, and body language. This anecdotal wisdom is borne out by the results from a Stanford School of Business Executive Coaching Survey that revealed the worst flaw in CEOs and other leaders is a lack of self-awareness. Without self-awareness, leaders are ill-equipped to set the right tone for their work culture and the lives they influence.

That's where business etiquette comes into the picture. Business etiquette is a mindset that underscores the importance of a winning combination: self-awareness and self-restraint. It's a vital tool that arms leaders with the business acumen to respond to others pragmatically and professionally, not emotionally and counterproductively. Practicing savvy etiquette and protocol suppresses the ego in favor of consideration for others and prioritizes the importance of making people around you feel respected, trusted, comfortable, and valued. Tone at the top matters. An *others–centered* mentality builds meaningful relationships and inspires talent so that bottom-line results occur in the form of new business, talent retention, and customer loyalty.

Heads Up, Leaders: Set yourself apart by equipping your toolbox with these essential, yet often overlooked, professional development skills. Is business etiquette a lost art? Only if meaningful relationship-building, authentic leadership, and high-caliber communication skills are outdated. In today's fiercely competitive marketplace, business etiquette is a smart way to invest in yourself and your career. Our world is rapidly changing, with technology and intercultural communication forging ahead with unprecedented force. One example is the geographic distribution of the remote workforce resulting from the pandemic, which impacts in-person encounters as well as more frequent behind-the-screen exchanges that in turn affects relationship-building. Corporate etiquette offers an essential roadmap to guide our behaviors as we nimbly adapt to a swiftly evolving professional landscape.

The result? Building relationship capital is the most important ingredient for career success. When one is keenly aware of how their behavior and words impact others, they understand how to make others feel comfortable, establish a professional presence, and motivate others to do their best work.

> Building relationship capital is the most important ingredient for career success.

In turn, a lifetime of dividends will come your way in the form of leadership opportunities, enhanced likeability, authenticity, and credibility as well as improved business performance.

Polished will help empower and equip you to become the finest ambassador of your employer and yourself you can be.

HOW TO READ THIS BOOK

Through the eye-opening lens of modern business etiquette, *Polished* is a unique compilation of 12 Building Blocks containing "pearls of wisdom" expertly designed to elevate one's professional development and business acumen.

Each Building Block includes 3 learning categories: ENGAGE, ENLIGHTEN, and ELEVATE.

They are as follows:

ENGAGE

Once upon a time,
unfortunate blunders were made . . .

Each Building Block opens by sharing the story of a common blunder that begs the question, "Could this be me?" A common mistake, awkward encounter, or frustration is relayed through a colorful character that could be you or someone you know.

ENLIGHTEN

with Ms. Tiffany's Epiphanies®

With a blunder or challenge identified, guidance is supplied to help you overcome it. Modern business etiquette and leadership guidance will help you navigate your career with power, professionalism, and poise. A strategy, tool, and/or alternative perspective to consider teaches you to course-correct and shift your behavior toward excellence for the betterment of career advancement. The goal behind each lesson is to empower you with etiquette and protocol intelligence so that others take notice.

ELEVATE

Learn by Doing Exercises

With skills in hand, it's time to apply them in real life. This is the critical juncture where the concepts merge into practicing each topic discussed in the Building Block. In a workbook format, you have the opportunity to complete exercises relevant to your own professional (and sometimes personal) life that deepen the meaning behind each lesson. These exercises are also designed to demonstrate how the topic at hand can reward even your most ambitious career aspirations. Learn by doing exercises turn information into knowledge that you can fluidly apply when it counts the most.

Principles of Professionalism (POP!)

The Power of Self-Awareness Part 1— Project More Confidence

ENGAGE

*Once upon a time,
unfortunate blunders were made . . .*

Have you ever missed the quiet signs of how you're presenting yourself in your career and how others are receiving you? Do you have a true read on the impact of your behavior, words, and body language? To be well-positioned, avoid becoming like the person you're about to meet. And if you encounter someone like him, run! Let me introduce to you Bentley Fosset, a wide-eyed Ivy League graduate, newly hired by a global data analytic enterprise. Bentley was raring to set the world on fire and make his indelible mark on society.

In high school and college, Bentley dazzled teachers and fellow classmates with his magnetic charisma and razor-sharp wit. Everything in life came easily to him, and he grew to expect success at every turn. This experience fed an expanding sense of entitlement that accolades and rapid advancement would come early and often in his career.

However, his inflated ego and quickness to brazenly respond to every mishap with self-assured hubris did not do him any favors when winning people over in the business world, as you'll see.

It was a frigid, blustery January morning on Bentley's first day at the global data firm, and his demeanor matched the weather. When he arrived at his workplace for new hire orientation, Bentley kicked off his rubber galoshes in disgust, muttering to himself under his breath. He had taken several wrong turns during his commute, almost making him late for his first day of work.

His foul mood still intact, Bentley sauntered into the meeting space exuding an air of superiority that ensured all forty attendees noticed him—and not in a positive way. Bentley approached the registration table, where he cut the line so *he* could vent his grievances. Rolling his eyes and spouting his displeasure in a thunderous voice as he clamored for a sympathetic ear to make *him* more comfortable only garnered even more negative attention.

Done complaining to the registration table personnel, Bentley grabbed a cup of coffee and, caustic self-obsession still firing on all cylinders, approached a cohort of new colleagues. They were engrossed in deep conversation, and their body language conveyed zero interest in welcoming a newcomer.

Naturally, Bentley interrupted them without hesitation. "Wow, you wouldn't believe my day so far! Is anyone else having a bad day?" Bentley continued without waiting for a reply, reciting his litany of unfortunate events.

One of the group members stepped up to explain to Bentley that they needed a few more minutes in private to finish discussing a plan to help a mutual friend in need. Bentley spoke over his new acquaintance, offering his unsolicited advice on their friend's circumstance.

In unison, each colleague attempted to calm themselves by:

- Touching their face (e.g., stroking a chin, rubbing eyebrows)
- Stroking the back of their neck
- Fiddling with their tie, collar, or hair
- Wringing their hands and biting their nails
- Twirling their hair or tucking hair behind their ears
- Crossing their arms in defiance
- Turning their feet and torso away

The agitated countenance of each member, coupled with broken eye contact, were dead giveaways that they would have preferred a root canal to having their discussion abruptly halted by a self-absorbed, discourteous new associate. Unsurprisingly, Bentley did not take the hints and proceeded to derail the conversation until the bell chimed for everyone to take their seats.

ENLIGHTEN

with Ms. Tiffany's Epiphanies®

Hello, my name is Self-Awareness.
(Not to be confused with my evil twin, Self-Absorption.)
We have not yet had the pleasure of meeting.

Every day of your career,
you and I should be side by side, bosom buddies.
I'm the nudge for you to be more observant of yourself,
pleading for your self-realization to spark.
I am the full-length mirror reflecting your true self,
which reveals how you are perceived.
Once we are better friends, you will set yourself apart.
Dare not be lulled into foolish belief that I am unimportant.
I am the distinction between how you read the room
and how the room reads you.
Dare not deny me, or I will deny you
in your quest for a higher self.

To be sure, Bentley is an extreme example. You may not feel like you ever exhibit this severity of poor behavior. However, meaningful lessons can be gleaned to heighten your self-awareness and diminish questionable, yet less consequential behaviors, that have the potential to damage your reputation and career advancement.

What skill would have enabled Bentley to make a more favorable impression? What character trait could ensure that *you* make the finest impression every time?

Successful leaders know this superpower well and own it. It's the power of *self-awareness*. Leaders of high distinction are living embodiments of self-awareness. They understand how to channel this superpower for good—to command respect, earn trust, persuade, and boost likeability.

NO ROOM FOR MEDIOCRITY

As a society, we are sadly moving away from a place of self-awareness and self-restraint. We are moving away from extending respect
and professional courtesy to one another. We are moving away from
feeling empathy toward others—the cornerstone of
meaningful relationship-building. We are moving away from the caring act of forgiveness
and toward the callous act of canceling
or ghosting others. To set yourself
apart from the masses, embrace modern business etiquette intelligence as
a career differentiator. With business
etiquette, there is no room for mediocrity. The foundational pillar behind
business etiquette is keen self-awareness.
We must understand ourselves and how
our words and behaviors impact others
before we can earn the trust of others and
navigate challenging situations seamlessly.

> **We must understand
> ourselves, and how
> our words and behaviors
> impact others before we
> can earn the trust of others
> and navigate challenging
> situations seamlessly.**

Define It

What is self-awareness? Self-awareness is the ability to focus on
yourself and how your actions, thoughts, or emotions do or don't
align with your internal standards. If you're highly self-aware, you
can objectively evaluate yourself, manage your emotions, align
your behavior with your values, and clearly understand the perceptions others have of you.

Revisiting the plight of poor Bentley, let's examine his top
three blunders and how a healthy dose of self-awareness could
have helped him create a better first impression.

1. "It's All About Me" Syndrome

Bentley's first misstep was about perspective—obviously, what mattered most to him was his comfort, emotions, and experiences, with no regard for anyone else. Etiquette intelligence seeks to suppress the ego in favor of empathetically prioritizing the needs of others over personal wants. In turn, when we help others, we're rewarded with trust, gratitude, and blossoming relationships.

If you give more than you take, you'll enter the winner's circle faster. Perhaps you are technologically proficient, and a senior leader is struggling with a social media app. Humbly offer to share your digital dexterity. Or perhaps you are the seasoned leader, a board member on community nonprofit boards. In that case, take an early career professional under your wing and teach them the ways of community board service. Addressing a personal need of someone's family member is a surefire way to become memorable and pull on another's heartstrings. For example, if an individual mentions that his son is having trouble securing an internship, offer to connect him with your centers of influence and follow through until you have exhausted your entire network. Gratitude bonds two people like nothing else.

2. Failure to Read and Project Proper Body Language

Bentley did not accurately read the room. His self-awareness was missing in action when it came to his own entrance—evidenced by his voice's caustic, grating volume and his insensitivity. Bentley also failed to notice that the group's body language was closed off and became increasingly distressed as he continued interjecting.

Aggressively kicking off his galoshes and murmuring his frustrations under his breath made Bentley a spectacle to behold. Be mindful about causing a distraction by calling negative attention to yourself. Your nonverbal social cues speak volumes and have the power to detonate an explosion of poor micro-impressions. Be cognizant of the room's serious or lighthearted vibe and your ability to seamlessly acclimate yourself to that vibe. Bentley should have made wiser choices, such as excusing himself to a private area to regain his composure, calling a trusted friend to vent, taking some cleansing breaths, or even doing a quick meditation or prayer.

When approaching a group, observe how direct and sustained the eye contact is between the conversation partners. Observe how squared their belly buttons and shoulders are to one another and how welcoming their facial expressions are. If the signs are pointing to a closed-off, intense private discussion, pivot to join another group that seems more open with their nonverbals. Finally, when approaching a group, seek one person to exchange smiles with while mouthing the words, "May I join you?" Use this connection as your gateway of entry into the group.

Our necks and faces are home to many nerve endings that, when touched, lower our heart rate and comfort us. When people are uncomfortable, they will unknowingly attempt to soothe their anxieties through self-touching. If you witness these self-calming gestures in someone with whom you are speaking, ask yourself, "What am I doing to cause them anxiety? How can I make this person more comfortable?"

Other people are not always adoring fans of everything we do. Whether in-person or on a social media platform, we don't have to sell front-row tickets to our less-than-proud moments. Go private when you're emotional—you'll regret less when your reputation is still intact and you've maintained your dignity.

3. Lack of Listening Skills and the Temptation to Interrupt

During conversation, does your mind wander? Are you anxiously waiting to intervene? Do you feel a yearning to spew your thoughts, even if what you're planning to say becomes irrelevant as the direction of the conversation pivots? You're not alone. This mistake is a prime example of what would happen if we married Blunder #1 (being me-focused) to Blunder #3 (lacking listening skills and rudely interrupting). The union would be far from blissful.

Interrupting others undermines how others view your competence. When we interrupt, we are viewed as having undeveloped people skills. Opt instead for focused, empathetic listening. There's a reason the words *listen* and *silent* are spelled with the same letters. Communication problems occur when we listen to reply rather than listen to understand.

> Communication problems occur when we listen to reply rather than listen to understand.

- Give the speaker your undivided attention. The gift of your presence is a present long remembered.

- Base your responses on your counterpart's two or three prior sentences, not on an agenda you prepared before the conversation started. Your interest will energize your listener.

The Power of Self-Awareness Part 2— Project More Credibility

ELEVATE

Learn by Doing Exercises

For the upcoming week, apply the lessons you learned to real life.

1. Self-Awareness Inventory

Grade yourself by checking the box:

- ☐ I have high self-awareness with a keen ability to read the room and pivot my behavior accordingly.

- ☐ I have above average self-awareness and can pivot my reactions pretty well.

- ☐ I have occasional self-awareness but am not consistent with my read or my competence in adjusting my behavior.

- ☐ I have minimal self-awareness and am not familiar with strategies needed to react to a challenging situation.

2. An Eye-Opening Exercise

Every day for a week, make a note of each person's eye color you encounter. You'll be surprised at how this exercise sharpens your powers of observation and improves your eye contact, making you more engaging.

3. Clueless Conundrums

Describe a scenario in which you observed a complete lack of self-awareness resulting in a poorly handled situation. Using this chapter's guidance, how could a heightened self-awareness have improved the outcome? Rewrite the scenario with a positive outcome.

The Power of Self-Restraint Part 1— Earn Trust in Leadership

ENGAGE

*Once upon a time,
unfortunate blunders were made . . .*

My name is Self-Restraint, not to be confused
with my chatty aunt, Loose Lips, who sinks ships.
I am the constant whisper that you often ignore.
Every day of your career, you and I should be inseperable,
setting sails on a voyage to combat regret.
I'm the nudge from inside your soul, pleading for you
to tether your unguarded tongue. I am the voice of
reason inside your head that when heard, suppresses
emotions to ensure a measured response and
to avoid inflammatory rhetoric. Once we are shipmates,

I am the anchor in the eye of the storm.
Dare not be lulled into foolish belief that I am unimportant.
I am the distinction between your calm and your turbulence.
I am your good taste, clear conscience,
and level of decorum. Dare not deny me, or I will
deny you in your quest for a controlled self.

Clutch my pearls! The following two scenarios evoke negative emotions. As you read, think about how you would handle each one.

TRIGGER #1: MAKE THE BOSS LOOK LIKE A FOOL. WAIT, WHAT?

At 8:02 a.m. on Monday morning, new hire Selma received an email that triggered a heated exchange with her boss. One of the PowerPoint (PPT) decks he had presented to the board included two slides from the wrong PPT, prematurely outing confidential information about a new product idea. His accusatory message ignited such an intense reaction that the thought crossed Selma's mind to hurl her laptop across the room and quit. Her boss was furious, yet misinformed, when he fired off this email:

Selma,

You are a genius. You are a genius at making me look like a fool. You included confidential information in the PPT deck about the unrevealed product to the board. They were so distracted by the slides that it led to the derailment of my entire presentation. Your carelessness prevented the board from making approvals for a critical deadline. I trusted you, but now I must clean up your mess.

Frank

A not-so-appropriate response:

Frank,

I did not insert those two slides. Your assistant did. I suggest getting your facts straight before unfairly attacking others who work tirelessly to make you look good. Maybe you could pick up the phone to ask me what happened before assuming I'm the fool?

Selma

A more appropriate response:

Frank,

It is disheartening to hear that there were PPT problems. I realize how important the success of this meeting was to you. Would you be open to discussing the mishap in person or over the phone? I may be better able to shed some light on what occurred, as I was not responsible for this error. Please let me know how I can be of assistance with damage control—I'm happy to help. It's critical that this never happens again so your presentations remain seamlessly executed with no surprises.

Sincerely,
Selma

Consider the windfall of positives that could occur with Selma's calmer response:

- Validated the boss's concerns

- Revealed the truth in a courteous, nonemotional manner showing professionalism and strong communication skills

- Exercised self-restraint by offering to discuss the issue in a format in which tone can be better read

- Exemplified a team player spirit by offering to repair the damage

- Offered empathy by declaring that this mistake should never repeat itself and why

- Reinforced her reputation for being a consummate professional who calmly solves problems during stressful times

TRIGGER #2: IT'S MY WAY OR THE HIGHWAY!

A high-end rug retailer took exception to their longstanding vendor's new policy requiring a deposit for any custom orders. The retailer pushed back, stating that their own policy is to pay vendors the full investment only after the delivery is received, so they can check first that it arrives in good condition:

Dear Mr. Rug Vendor,

Please understand that our corporate vendor policy states that all orders must be received in good condition before payment is made. It takes several months to generate the payment since our accounts payable department is back-logged. You know we are good for the payment.

High-End Retailer

A not-so-appropriate response:

Dear Mr. High-End Retailer,

Our new policy requires a deposit before any custom order can be started. It is what it is, so like it or not, we are not budging. No exceptions. This has never posed a problem with any other customer, and we resent you bullying us. Make a decision then let us know.

Rug Vendor

A more appropriate response:

Dear Mr. High-End Retailer,

We appreciate your concern. I wish I could accommodate your request as you are an important customer, and we have always valued our long-term partnership. A deposit is required since goods need to be ordered and this ensures our cash flow needs are met. We will still need to request a deposit before the order is started. Perhaps we can explore different timing for the delivery to better align with your cash needs. Would that be helpful? Let's schedule a call to discuss. Thank you for your understanding and patience.

With appreciation,
Rug Vendor

ENLIGHTEN

with Ms. Tiffany's Epiphanies®

DOUSE THE FIERY TONGUE AND STASH THE FERVID TYPING FINGERS

A thought-provoking quote delivered at an opportune moment enriches life and teaches valuable lessons. The following four quotes will inspire you to embrace the importance of restraining your fiery tongue and tucking your fervid typing fingers into your pockets. The key to honing the skill of self-restraint depends on your competence in extracting (or at least minimizing) the emotion when you are triggered. Suppressing an emotional response is difficult but worth it. When you exercise self-control, you open the door to calm, rational problem solving and critical thinking.

Quote #1

> "You will continue to suffer if you have an emotional reaction to everything that is said to you. True power is sitting back and observing things with logic. True power is restraint. If words control you, that means everyone else can control you. Breathe and allow things to pass."

—OFTEN ATTRIBUTED TO WARREN BUFFETT

Warren Buffett is worth billions, so it's fair to conclude that he knows something about business success. In fact, Buffett knows what it takes to surge ahead of his competition. This leader's sage advice is full of wisdom and smart business acumen. If we heed his warning, far less regret and wasteful consternation over a regrettable rant will result.

Quotes #2 and #3

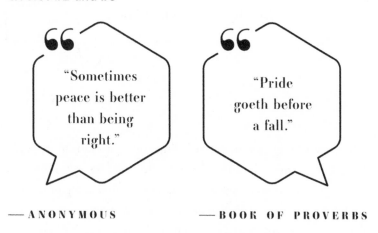

"Sometimes peace is better than being right."

—ANONYMOUS

"Pride goeth before a fall."

—BOOK OF PROVERBS

Being right at all costs produces loss. This loss manifests itself in the absence of humility, trust, self-esteem, productivity, energy, reputation, and most importantly, relationships. Before you're triggered to react inappropriately, save yourself by asking:

- What will I gain from being right?

- Is there another way to protect myself from being treated wrongly or disrespectfully?

If you're striving to always win the fight by proving your case, this quest can generate prideful or self-righteous arrogance.

Arrogance alienates. Ask yourself first if making the other person feel smaller, weaker, or wrong is worth being right.

Quote #4

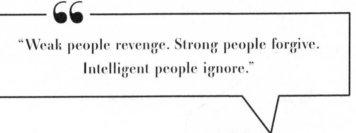

"Weak people revenge. Strong people forgive. Intelligent people ignore."

— ALBERT EINSTEIN

There are times when firmly standing your ground is justified, as long as it's done with professional courtesy and respect. However, making the conscious decision to actively ignore antagonism and not allow anger to reign remains a sound strategy in maintaining power and control. Breathe and allow things to pass.

We All Make Mistakes—Period

Nobody is perfect, and there are always three sides to every story—each party's version and the truth, which lies somewhere in the middle. We've all said regrettable things when emotions were running high and wished we could press rewind to take back our words. What says more about your character is how you handle yourself *after* you wrong someone.

When we make a verbal blunder, an opportunity presents itself to learn from that blunder and treat others better the next time. Apologizing and taking full responsibility are admirable measures of courage and the purest form of vulnerability. Once you feel remorse over the pain you caused, you should get to work making it right. In turn, when facing the headwinds of a person who has wronged you, even more than once, it takes great humility and character to rethink your hardline stance and find forgiveness in your heart. What goes around comes around, and when the shoe is inevitably on the other foot someday, you'll be glad you took the high road of forgiveness.

Show Yourself Compassion: As important as it is to show grace to others, it's equally important to show grace to yourself when you make mistakes. Appreciate yourself and realize that the word *fail* also means *First Attempt in Learning*. The word *no* also means *Next Opportunity*.

The Power of Self-Restraint Part 2— Exude a More Powerful You

ELEVATE

Learn by Doing Exercises

1. The Toothpaste Challenge

Recruit your colleagues or friends to take this challenge. Then, the next time you're triggered and on the slippery slope of losing self-control, recall this poignant, sticky visual, and you'll have fewer regrets. Organize a group into two smaller groups. Hold up the prize money. Explain that you are the timekeeper, and they have two minutes to compete. Direct one member of each group to squirt toothpaste onto a paper plate. The others then must race to be the first team to return all the paste back into the tube. When time is up, declare no winner and conclude that it's impossible to put the paste back in the tube, just as it's impossible to put regrettable words back into our mouths like they've never been spewed. The same logic may be applied to posting anything on the internet or social media. Once the toothpaste comes out of the tube, such as an online post or an email, it's difficult to get it back in the tube again.

What Happens When the Toothpaste Squeezes Out of the Tube?

The reality is that humans make mistakes, and inevitably, we all let the toothpaste out of the tube and wish we hadn't. Nonetheless, there is a higher, more divine principle that overrides the good secular practice taught in The Toothpaste Challenge: *forgiveness*. Forgiveness is the greatest form of love humans have to offer. Once a person leans into the merits of forgiveness, a chain reaction of goodness in living is kindled in the lives of all involved. Forgiveness releases the toxicity inherent from holding a grudge. Never be above the admirable act of forgiveness and miss an opportunity to take the high road and extend grace. As my grandfather would say, "No matter how flat the pancake is, there are always two sides to it." The grace you give to another human (and the liberating peace felt from giving it) says more about your character, integrity, stability, and heart than anything else. It's always more civil and humane to walk the compassionate path forward. How many times should we forgive? Not seven times, but seventy times seven, according to the Book of Matthew. Forgiving doesn't mean erasing harm done; it's just releasing your resentment toward the wrongdoer, regardless of whether or not they deserve this gift. Taking the high road doesn't mean keeping your forgiveness hidden in your heart. It means sharing your forgiveness with the wrongdoer and trying to find a healthier connection with that person. Be prepared to be pleasantly surprised with the karma you create when you forgive—the goodness that replaces the bitterness invites far more positivity and peace into your life.

Few people live to regret it when they forgive, but many do ask themselves why they didn't do it sooner.

Few people live to regret it when they forgive, but many do ask themselves why they didn't do it sooner.

2. Press Rewind—Fast-Forward to a More Powerful You

Recall a past exchange where your response was hostile and did not represent your finest moment.

- Write down the story detailing your regrettable reaction. Which of the four quotes in this chapter could have rescued you from regret?

- Press the rewind button and rewrite the story with what you wished you had (or had not) said.

- Which of the four quotes resonated the most with you? Which will improve your reaction when you are triggered? Jot down your favorite quote, memorize it, and create a daily reminder on your smartphone.

Favorable First Impressions

Elevate Your Likeability

Once upon a time,
unfortunate blunders were made . . .

Susie Chap and David Drier were competing for the sales job of their dreams at renowned candy manufacturing company Spittle Spattles. The company's HR director noticed that each had enough experience to be the next rainmaker in sales for the organization.

Susie showed up bubbly and vivacious, projecting confidence and positivity. David arrived more laid-back in demeanor, with his hands in his pockets and a go-with-the-flow attitude easily mis-construed as indifference. The favored choice for this coveted role seemed like a no-brainer—until the candidates started talking.

When Susie spoke, she barely paused for breath, and her sing-song up-speak was nauseating. Her voice rose in inflection at the end of each sentence as if she were posing a question for approval or appeasement. This habit undermined her credibility and sounded like screeching nails on a chalkboard to the HR director. When questioned about the distracting habit, Susie grew defensive and dismissed the inquiry. She then mentally checked out. Her stature shrank as she crossed her arms and legs and hunched her shoulders, pulling her elbows in close to her sides. Her furrowed brow and stern frown revealed brewing resentment.

David had a different attitude, garnering much likeability. He answered each interview question thoughtfully while sharing engaging stories that validated his track record and pulled at the interviewer's heartstrings. When the HR director pointed out that David's leg had been shaking nonstop during the interview, David blushed, quipping that he was guilty as charged and was working to eliminate this nervous tic. He grinned earnestly, thanking the director for bringing this to his attention so he could continue his quest to quell the habit.

Unsurprisingly, David was offered the job because of his likeability, not to mention coachability. The director was drawn to his ability to perform under pressure.

ENLIGHTEN

with Ms. Tiffany's Epiphanies®

Hello, my name is Likeability,
not to be confused with my deplorable sister, Repulsion.
We have not yet had the pleasure of meeting.
For the duration of your career, you and
I should be faithful friends, winning people over.
I'm the charm that endears you to others,

beckoning you to become a team player,
bringing out the best in all.
Once you and I grow tighter, you become irresistible,
and my worth ceases to be underestimated.
Dare not be lulled into foolish belief that I am unimportant.
I am a must-have, not a nice-to-have, when it comes to your
advancement. I am the distinction from
dull and ho-hum . . . your doorman to opportunity.
Dare not deny me, or I will deny you and
your quest for an alluring self.

ARE YOU LIKED AT YOUR WORKPLACE?

Why does the winning trifecta of likeability, trust, and respect make us unstoppable in our career pursuits? Likeable people inspire productivity. They network with ease. They promote harmony and fun in the workplace. They bring out the best in others. Likeability matters when it counts the most, such as when a job interview surfaces, a leadership opportunity presents itself, or a promotion becomes imminent on the horizon.

THE LIKEABILITY RULE

Nonverbal communication speaks the loudest. In the 1970s, UCLA Professor Albert Mehrabian made a remarkable revelation. He concluded that we size up others by placing greater weight on their nonverbal cues and less weight on spoken words. Quantifiably, Mehrabian assigned likeability percentages to three behaviors: 55% weight to body language, 38% weight to voice, and only 7% weight to spoken words. Hence, nonverbal cues (body language and voice) are more important than the words we say.[1]

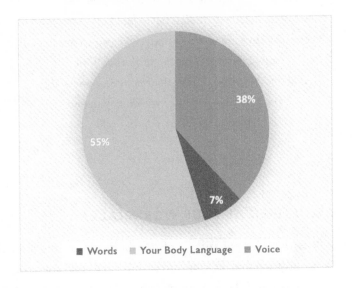

WHILE WE'RE HERE

If a person's gestures are incongruent with their spoken words, trust their gestures for the real read. For example, if someone says that they are comfortable around you but nervously twirls their hair while they speak, the truth lies in their self-soothing gestures, not their words. Etiquette intelligence should center on both accurately projecting and reading nonverbal cues. Body language serves as a secret decoder equipping you with invaluable

---

[1] Albert Mehrabian, *Silent Messages* (Belmont, CA: Wadsworth Publishing Company, 1971).

clues to read the situation and potentially pivot your behavior for the optimal result.

Blunder #1: Susie's Likeability Drops by 55%

Your body language has the power to be your best friend or worst foe. According to the Likeability Rule, Susie lost the job offer because she put 55% of her likeability in jeopardy due to her defiant body language.

Susie's defiant body language did not do her any favors. On the other hand, it's worth mentioning that even if she evinced no expressions, the absence of supportive body language would have reduced her likeability. Be mindful of *deadpan nonverbals* when faces are expressionless and gestures are unanimated. This likewise negatively impacts 55% of a person's likeability. Gestures must underscore our messaging. While listening, express through facial gestures that you're interested. Nodding in threes at opportune moments, smiling softly, and opening your eyes wider for emphasis can all empower you to be a highly effective conversationalist.

Blunder #2: Susie's Likeability Drops by 38%

Unless you have a voice like Morgan Freeman, be mindful of **The 4 Ps of Vocal Variation:**

1. **Pace:** The pace of speech greatly impacts how you're perceived. Speaking rapidly is a more common bad habit than speaking too slowly, but both extremes cause negative impressions. If you are consistently asked to repeat yourself, consider it a red flag to address. Slow down, project your

voice, and enunciate clearly. Nobody wants to be forced to work hard to understand you. Likewise, when we speak too slowly, we are inclined to lose the listener's attention or chase them away due to annoyance. Be careful never to use your pace to speak condescendingly to a person. This is a temptation when a listener does not appear to understand what we're saying. To dramatically enunciate too slowly and emphatically to make the other person understand you is off-putting and in poor form.

2. **Pitch:** Pitch is defined as how high or low our vocal frequencies range when we talk. Susie's high pitch undermined her credibility. There's a reason Margaret Thatcher underwent vocal training before she became prime minister: She believed it would help her advance in her political aspirations. When a man's voice is low, a common perception is that he is dominant and capable, both traits of strong leaders. When a woman's voice is high, especially when up-speak is employed, she is perceived as weak and someone who should be taken less seriously.

3. **Projection:** Projection is the strength and volume by which the sound of your voice is heard. You may recall the *Puffy Shirt* episode of Seinfeld, where Kramer is dating a red-haired low-talker. She is repeatedly asked to repeat herself by Jerry and Elaine over dinner. When the sound of the low-talker's voice remains muffled, they give up trying to understand her. If your projection is habitually weak, others will dismiss you as frustrating or insecure since it requires too much work to understand you.

4. **Pause:** There is power in the pause. When you pause, attention is diverted right back to you. Use this tactic if you lose someone's attention. The pause also creates a dramatic notion that what you're saying is poignant. So by all means, pause for poise and power.

Secret Voice Weapons for Commanding Respect

A Personal Share: When I need to be taken seriously, I alter my pitch, especially at the end of my sentences, and slow my pace down, placing careful emphasis on the phrases that most strongly support my messaging and intent. It's interesting what Morgan Freeman recommended about lowering his voice to its natural level. He said, "If you're looking to improve the sound of your voice, yawn a lot. It relaxes your throat muscles. It relaxes your vocal cords. And as soon as they relax, the tone drops. The lower your voice is, the better you sound."[2]

---

[2] Mandy Oaklander, "Science Explains Why You Love Morgan Freeman's Voice," *Time Magazine*, February 23, 2016.

Discard Distracting Verbal Fillers: Uh, Like, Kinda, Ya Know

ENGAGE

Once upon a time,
unfortunate blunders were made . . .

Hello, I would like to introduce myself as
a pesky Verbal Filler, (uh) not to be confused
with my silver-tongued nephew, Eloquence.
(So) every day of your career, you and I should (kinda)
avoid each other like the plague. I'm the annoyance
that (sort of) distracts from your (um) message.
I scream to the (uh) world, "Help! I am lost!
I need more time for my (um) brain to (ya know)
catch up with my words." When noticed,
people are (sort of) distracted and
perturbed (and whatnot). Once you and I dissociate,
the fluency of your speech will be smooth as glass.
Silence becomes golden as the pause becomes your new friend.

*Dare not be lulled into foolish belief that my presence is
inconsequential. Indeed, if you do not extract me from your speech,
(like) my wrath will take aim at your precious reputation (Right?).*

ENLIGHTEN

with Ms. Tiffany's Epiphanies®

The quickening pace of our ever-evolving technology landscape
and the rise of remote work in the wake of the COVID-19 pandemic indicate that many of us will be communicating more and
more through screens. Poor vocal habits form more easily over vid-
eoconference meetings, so without discipline in our vocal habits,
we will project less intelligence while revealing more insecurities.

Verbal fillers (e.g., *so, um, like, well, kind of, uh, stuff, you know,
right?*) undermine our credibility as thoughtful conversationalists
or eloquent orators. We insert these verbal hiccups to allow our
brains time to catch up with our mouths. They scream to the
world, "I'm not confident about my message!" Some mistakenly
believe verbal fillers are only used by the young, but these distractors transcend all ages. I know a middle-aged teacher who
consistently asks her students, "You know what I mean?" She
has no idea she is detracting from her own lessons. Be careful
about falling into the trending trap of using the distracting filler
phrase *and whatnot* when listing other things of a similar kind.
For example, "There's an amazing app that will help you organize
by artist, playlist, podcast, and whatnot."

So long, *so*: Several prominent business leaders strongly suggested that I offer this word of caution about a trending fad of
starting too many explanations with the word *so*. They are frustrated
with how this tiny word has become unnecessarily commonplace

and annoyingly distracting. Beginning a sentence with *so* has propelled it to become the new *like* or *sort of.* This peeve wasn't around years ago but has reared its ugly head, dominating today's conversations and explanations. You might ask, "What's the big deal?" And to your point, not everyone cares about the use of *so.* However, the ones who are annoyed by it care a great deal. People are misusing this word as a verbal crutch to introduce a new topic, perhaps to buy time to gather their thoughts. Additionally, *so* is often misused at the beginning of an explanation to provide context or background. An overuse of this word not only undermines your credibility as an intelligent speaker, but it also may be off-putting to those who feel like you are exerting an air of superiority in sharing your knowledge. It can be (wrongly or rightly) perceived as condescending in an attempt to make others feel less equal. Think of an alternative way to begin a sentence or, better yet, skip using this extraneous word altogether and get right to the point.

WORDS MATTER: SPEAK WITH AUTHORITY

We are delusional in thinking that we will miraculously self-correct when a high-pressure situation ensues. On the contrary, that is the precise time annoying habits rear their ugly heads as our nerves take over. Break the habit with these five strategies:

1. **Pause.** Gathering one's thoughts is what Ralph Richardson meant when he concluded in a quote often attributed to him, "The most precious things in speech are the pauses." Silence is golden, and the pause is your friend. Well-timed pauses harness impact and draw attention back to you.

2. **Recruit an Accountability Partner.** Ask a trusted friend to track the number of times you depend on fillers so you can hold yourself accountable.

3. **Join Toastmasters International.** When it comes to public speaking finesse, this organization is brilliant at helping members become competent communicators. They offer opportunities to practice strategies in a safe and encouraging forum. A portion of their evaluation process involves counting the frequency of your fillers to sharpen your self-awareness.

4. **Prepare and Avoid Overpacking.** Today's preparation guarantees tomorrow's achievements. If you are well-prepared with solid content, people will inadvertently turn their attention to what you are saying, not how you are saying it. You will naturally slow down and take breaths, so the fillers won't creep in. Avoid packing excessive amounts of material into a presentation or a conversation, and avoid the temptation to rapid-fire your content to meet a time constraint. This is prime breeding ground for fillers.

5. **Be Brief. Be Brilliant. Be Gone.** Longer sentences filled with unnecessary words get us into trouble. Use simple, forceful sentences, with one subject and one verb.

Half of the battle is realizing that these verbal villains do indeed creep into our speech through the side door. Practice these strategies, and enjoy blossoming into a well-spoken, articulate communicator who leaves an impeccable lasting impression.

ELEVATE

Learn by Doing Exercise

Implement the five strategies outlined in the prior section. Pause more, recruit a verbal filler counter, and attend your local Toastmasters chapter (it's free!). Streamline your content and make it succinct.

Handshake Fails and Flops

ENGAGE

Once upon a time,
unfortunate blunders were made . . .

As the world heals from the sickness, death, and despair of the COVID-19 pandemic, our society has adapted to becoming more touchless. Sadly, we've pressed pause on the casual handshakes and hugs we used to give so freely. Even Kentucky Fried Chicken's beloved sixty-four-year-old slogan, *Finger Lickin' Good*, was temporarily suspended for leaving a bad taste in the mouths of its loyal patrons.

A Personal Share: I am quite optimistic that hugs and handshakes will fully return to their former place of glory. These greetings, which date back thousands of years, are too entrenched in our culture to not return. They represent connection and acceptance and help establish a bit about who we are, from our personal warmth and comfort to our style of leadership and business acumen.

At the onset of any greeting—before uttering a word—your handshake makes the first and loudest impression. Research reveals that it takes about three hours of human interaction to establish the same amount of rapport as one handshake. An engaging connection is optimized when eye contact is sustained, facial expression is welcoming, grip pressure is equal, and pressed hands are aligned. To avoid making a poor impression, keep an eye on these **5 Worst Handshake Fails:**

1. **The Bonecrusher.** When grip pressure is excessively forceful, a person is striving to exert their dominance and superiority. How should you react to this painful approach? Disarm them (well, not literally) by releasing any pressure in your hand and they will do the same.

2. **The Stiff-Arm Thrust.** When someone extends a stiff arm and has no bend at the elbow, a person is distancing themselves from you. Celebrities and public figures are classic violators. The thrust occurs when the movement is made in the shoulder. A proper handshake has the movement centered in the elbow area only.

3. **The Wimpy Dead Fish.** When someone weakly clasps the tips of your fingers, a person is exuding submissiveness or discounting the importance of your encounter. However, when greeting a person from another culture—such as Korea, Africa, the Caribbean—a firm handshake is not the norm and may be considered rude. That said, this book only covers Westernized culture, though my company— Cincinnati Etiquette & Leadership Institute, LLC—offers cultural awareness and international protocol instruction.

4. **The Glove.** When someone piles on by simultaneously touching the arm of another as they are shaking their hand,

it's too intimate since personal space is invaded. In the business world, there's no place for this intimacy. Save the extra love for Sunday dinners at Grandma's house.

5. **The Milkshake.** When someone pumps excessively to the point that the handshake never seems to end, that person does not know when enough is enough. This can be exhausting.

ENLIGHTEN

with Ms. Tiffany's Epiphanies®

The exact origin of the handshake has a question mark in the history books but most likely dates back thousands of years to Greece. Viewed as a gesture of peace, the handshake is used in friendship, business, cultural exchanges, and religious traditions. Back in the day, a popular theory was that the handshake was a litmus test to protect you from untrustworthy, weapon-carrying scoundrels. By pumping hands, handshakers checked if a weapon was being carried by dislodging any weaponry hidden in a sleeve.

Today, handshakes are a sign of respect and connection when done properly. Therefore, be mindful of these **6 Handshake Best Practices:**

1. **Be the Initiator.** The person who extends their hand first establishes control and has a distinct advantage.

2. **The Dual Pump.** Two smooth, firm pumps is the recommended protocol in a Westernized society. That quantity varies in other countries.

3. **Web to Web.** Go all the way in when shaking. Press your web, the area between your thumb and index finger, against the other person's web.

4. **Square Up and Swoosh.** Similar to a basketball player squaring up to the hoop to take the shot, you should square up with your counterpart navel to navel and shoulder to shoulder when shaking hands to fully engage. If your torso or feet are angled away, you are broadcasting a signal that you wish to be anywhere else.

5. **Stand Up.** It's not proper form to remain seated while shaking a person's hand. Show respect by standing up when you shake hands.

6. **Clear the Way.** When shaking hands, remove any obstacles, such as a table or even other people, between you and your counterpart. If you are meeting members in a group, move around the circle so that you are squared up and directly facing each person, giving them your undivided attention for a few seconds.

ELEVATE

Learn by Doing Exercise

Make impeccable first and last impressions during handshaking with these six best practices in exercising common courtesy:

1. Be the Initiator.

2. The Dual Pump.

3. Web to Web.

4. Square Up and Swoosh.

5. Stand Up.

6. Clear the Way.

Distinguished Dining in the Professional World

ENGAGE

Once upon a time,
unfortunate blunders were made . . .

MY DREAM JOB

Son: "Mom, great news! I crushed my first three on-campus interviews, and the recruiter called to inform me that I am advancing to the fourth and final round! The last round is a two-day process in Chicago where the first night is a dinner with several recruiters and about twenty-five candidates, and the second day is five hours of interviews. Of course, the most important day is the day of interviews and not the dinner."

Mom: "Son, you have it backwards. The recruiters will be judging you with keener scrutiny in the dining room since this is a new experience. This isn't the time to let your guard down since being competent at the dining table for business is just another form of interviewing you."

Was the son correct in saying that the interview meetings were more important than the dinner? Mom clutches her pearls and thinks not. She would be right on this one. The son's potential employer is already impressed with his interview skills or he wouldn't have advanced to the final round. The reason the company is hosting a dinner is to ascertain whether the son is savvy enough to be trusted over a meal with their senior management, valued clients, and other centers of influence.

While We're Here: After the final round of interviews, the next day, the son was driving back to campus and informed his mom that he would send a thank-you note to the recruiter the following week. Instead, the mom insisted that he pull over at a gas station and email a thank-you message to the recruiter the very day the interviews concluded. The son begrudgingly relented and followed his mom's advice. Three hours later, the recruiter called to say the thank-you email had come through on his phone just as he was sitting around a table of recruiters trying to decide which candidates would receive job offers. The recruiter said he had read the son's thank-you note, which was specific in detail and bountiful in gratitude, aloud to the rest of the recruiters. Everyone gathered agreed that if the son had that kind of professional courtesy and those kind of high behavioral standards, he should receive an offer hands-down. The mom then reminded the son to also put a handwritten thank-you note in the mail the following week for good measure. (A thank-you email is perfectly acceptable on its own nowadays, but when the stakes are high, don't hesitate to go the extra mile and follow up the email with a handwritten note as well.) Rare professional courtesy and respect pay off in the workplace!

ENLIGHTEN

with Ms. Tiffany's Epiphanies®

TABLE FOR TWO? A FAVORABLE FIRST IMPRESSION IS RIGHT THIS WAY . . .

Have a seat at the table to learn the difference between the art of dining and the act of eating. When there is business to conduct in the dining room, you want to represent your employer and yourself with class to make the finest impression. The goal at a business meal is to move fluidly and seamlessly through the meal while keeping your guest engaged. Stay on point with the business agenda at hand, while having brilliant conversation. When you make etiquette gaffes at a business meal, you may never know why you didn't secure the job, why you didn't impress the client, or why you didn't win the deal. Often, we don't realize we are even making these blunders. We eat in a manner and style taught to us by our parents or guardians in the relaxed setting of our home, but when we enter formal occasions, there is a higher expectation of etiquette, manners, and self-awareness.

It's hard to go wrong if you keep the following in mind:

THE TOP 6 DINING DOs

1. **Do show waitstaff courtesy** with eye contact and use *please* and *thank you.* Stow handbags out of the way under your chair to show consideration so the waitstaff doesn't trip. Begin requests with, "Whenever you have a free moment, would you mind . . ."

2. **Do wait for others to be served before lifting your utensils to eat.** This shows patience and respect for others at the table rather than a rush to devour.

3. **Do cut and convey one bite at a time** instead of cutting all the food at once. This prevents your plate from resembling your dog's breakfast bowl.

4. **Do pass the bread and condiments to the right.** If they are located close to you, it's your responsibility to initiate the passing. It's polite to offer the bread to the person on your left (without letting go of the bread bowl) but then explain that you will be passing it to the right once they take a piece.

5. **Do keep elbows, forearms, and napkin off the table.** There are never uncooked joints on the table while eating, no matter how tired you feel.

6. **Do place your silverware in the proper finishing position.** When you are finished with your meal, place your fork and knife parallel in the center of your plate. Imagine the 10:00 and 4:00 on the face of a clock. Place the utensils close together, with tines up and knife blade pointed toward you.

TOP 6 TABLE TABOOS

1. **Don't pass the salt and pepper separately.** The shakers are *married* and must stay together, even if only one is requested. Do not salt your food before tasting it, as this is considered an offense to the chef's culinary skills.

2. **Don't eat quickly without properly chewing your food (small bites).** A formal meal is to be enjoyed by savoring the food and conversation. Rushing is disrespectful to the

enjoyment of others. It's important to adapt to the same pace of eating as the other diners at your table. Avoid having *chipmunk cheeks* by not chewing in small bites. Small bites allow you to answer questions promptly.

3. **Don't place your silverware on the table once you have used the utensil.** This includes resting one end of the utensil on the plate and the other end on the table. Used silverware should always rest on the plate and never touch the table again.

4. **Don't hold the wine glass by its bowl.** It's called stemware for a reason. It's proper form to hold the glass stem. This exudes sophistication, but also protects the wine's temperature, ultimately affecting its flavor. Holding the stem also prevents smudging the glass to ensure a cleaner look.

5. **Don't hunch over the table.** Poor posture does not project authority and makes you look like you have low energy or are indifferent. Sit up and lean in slightly so that the silhouette of your back and the back of the chair is V-shaped.

6. **Don't cut your meat like a caveman.**

   - **Cutting:** If right-handed, hold the knife in your right hand with your index finger on the handle, overlapping the blade no more than one inch for leverage in cutting. Hold the fork in your left hand, tines down. Avoid the caveman in the Stone Age look—do not pierce the meat with your left fist clenched around the fork and proceed to cut with your right hand. This is a common blunder that draws negative attention.

   - **After cutting:** Rest the knife angled on the upper right corner of the plate. The blade's cutting edge faces inward toward the center of the plate. Switch the fork to your right hand before raising it to your mouth. Avoid being a distraction by loudly clanging the silverware on the plate. Hold the fork in your right hand like a pencil, steadied between the index finger and middle finger. Ensure that elbows are tucked in at your sides during the cutting motion.

ELEVATE

Learn by Doing Exercises

- **The Dozen Donut Directive:** Purchase a dozen donuts (tough job, but someone has to do it!) and practice the cutting technique.

- **The Oops Log:** Heighten your self-awareness by observing the Dining Dos and Table Taboos in real life. For three weeks, maintain a daily log of violations made by your family, friends, restaurant patrons, and yourself. After mulling over the list of dining missteps, you'll think twice about committing them yourself when it matters most.

The Art of Meaningful Relationship- Building

The Power of Empathy
Part 1

ENGAGE

Once upon a time,
unfortunate blunders were made . . .

Hello, my name is Empathy, not to
be confused with my callous cousin, Apathy.
I've been looking forward to getting to know you better.
Every day of your career, you and I should be soulmates,
tying your compassion to another's struggle.
I'm the nudge from inside your heart,
from inside your gut pleading for you to listen more,
feel more, care more. I am the voice inside your head
that when heard, helps you step into someone else's shoes
(even if they're not your size). Once we become closer,
the perspective of your former self shifts.

Dare not be lulled into foolish belief that I am unimportant.
I am the catalyst behind proper behaviors in life.
Dare not deny me, or I will deny you the driving force of what
will make your relationships and interactions thrive.

As I was writing this book, the world witnessed jaw-dropping milestones as the COVID-19 pandemic impacted our health, healthcare system, economy, and collective mental health. But there is another age-old *virus* that continues to wreak havoc on humanity and the ability of some to recognize that all people are created equal. That virus is the prejudice and bigotry that causes racial injustice. If only we would employ the power of empathy in race relations! Empathy tragically remains an untapped resource in the quest to unify humanity.

The following story is a powerful illustration of true empathy. This story, taken from history, artfully depicts how transformative empathy can be in opening hearts and bonding the souls of two different humans, ultimately conquering hate.

"Claiborne Paul Ellis was born into a poor white family in North Carolina, in 1927. Finding it hard to make ends meet and believing African Americans were the cause of his trouble, he followed his father's footsteps and joined the Ku Klux Klan, rising to the top of his KKK branch. In 1971, he was invited to a 10-day community meeting to tackle racial tensions in schools and was chosen to head a steering committee with Ann Atwater, a Black activist he despised. He soon discovered that she shared the same problems of poverty as his own. 'I was beginning to look at a Black person, shake hands with him, and see him as a human being. It was like being born again.' On the final night of the meeting, he stood in front of a thousand people and tore up his Klan membership card. Ellis became a labor organizer for a union whose membership was 70% African American. He and Ann remained friends for the rest of their lives."[3]

Years later, when Ellis died from complications due to Alzheimer's at seventy-eight, Ann Atwater delivered his eulogy at the funeral.

An inclusive corporate culture with high levels of empathy would significantly empower the fight against racial inequality. Research from Bersin by Deloitte's IMPACT 2017 conference in Florida presented these findings: "Organizations with inclusive cultures are six times more likely to be innovative . . . to anticipate change and respond effectively, and twice as likely to meet or exceed financial targets. [However,] only 2% of organizations around the world have reached full maturity [potential]." As the song goes, "What the world needs now is love" . . . like never before.

ENLIGHTEN

with Ms. Tiffany's Epiphanies®

The internet and electronic devices have radically redefined how we all communicate. Sadly, mediocrity is prevailing, and we are becoming crasser and more casual with our expressions, thus

[3] Kyle MacDonald, "Are You In or Are You Out?," *Psychotherapist*, April 27, 2013.

compromising meaningful relationship-building. A society-wide reduction in empathy is the root cause. Empathy is one of the driving forces behind proper behaviors and successful relationships.

As Roman Krznaric, empathy consultant and founding faculty member of The School of Life, notes:

> The 20th century was the Age of Introspection . . . but it left us gazing at our own navels . . . The 21st century should become the Age of Empathy, when we discover ourselves not simply through self-reflection, but by becoming interested in the lives of others. We need empathy to create a new kind of revolution in human relationships.[4]

However, according to the *Financial Times*, we are suffering, not just from a reduction in empathy, but from an empathy deficit:

> Our interconnected world has never had lonelier, more angry people. Is technology responsible for a decline in human empathy? **Levels of empathy fell by 48% between 1979 and 2009.** Possible causes of the growing empathy gap include increasing materialism, changing parenting methods, and the digital echo chamber, in which people anchor themselves in close-knit groups of like-minded people.[5]

---

[4] Roman Krznaric, "Six Habits of Highly Empathic People," *Greater Good Magazine*, November 27, 2012, https://greatergood.berkeley.edu/article/item/six_habits_of_highly_empathic_people1.

[5] Zurich Insurance Group, "Decline in Human Empathy Creates Global Risks in the 'Age of Anger,'" *Financial Times*, https://biggerpicture.ft.com/cyber-risk/article/decline-human-empathy-creates-global-risks-age-anger/, accessed February 25, 2022.

Empathy differentiates. Empathy enlightens. Empathy commiserates. Empathy amplifies. Empathy energizes. Empathy supports. Empathy encourages. Empathy validates. Empathy resonates. Empathy engages. Empathy penetrates. Empathy elevates.

WHAT IS YOUR EMPATHY LEVEL?

> "As a leader, you should always start with where people are before you try to take them where you want them to go."

— JIM ROHN, ENTREPRENEUR AND AUTHOR

Empathy is similar to a muscle that needs to be exercised to grow stronger. A leader's arsenal contains many skills, but empathy is key. Empathy is often dismissed as a feel-good, soft, and fuzzy trait that is lovely to have but not essential to success. This is nonsense and a misguided notion. If empathy is lacking in a workplace, then so is employee engagement, morale, relationship-building, productivity, and bottom-line results.

When we lack empathy, we lack the depth of emotional intelligence and the ability to authentically lead and relate to others.

Define It

Empathy is a perspective shift that allows you to walk in the shoes of another person, understanding and validating their needs or emotional state for the goal of using this newly learned understanding to guide, and pivot, your own behavior in response.

Empathy connects your heart to the heart of others and leaves no room for your personal agenda or self-interest. Be careful—empathy is not to be confused with sympathy. Sympathy is the superficial act of feeling pity, avoiding the hard work of connecting to another's emotional state and experience. Which response inspires a deeper connection?

- A sympathetic response: "Wow, bummer. Good luck with that. At least you have one parent who's still alive. You're tough and will be just fine."

- An empathetic response: "That must be so difficult. I hear you and can relate. I felt overwhelmed by a similar pain with my family a couple of years ago. Know that if you ever want to talk about it, I'm here for you and care—seriously."

We use empathy to mourn a loss or celebrate a win. We venture beyond our own ego to say *I'm sorry* or *congratulations* because we don't have to be the center of attention and another's win is not our loss.

Replies That Lack Empathy

- Trust me, I have been there and know exactly how you feel.

- Time heals all wounds, and you will be just fine.

- I figured you'd get the promotion.

- You're better off knowing now. It could be worse.

- Everything happens for a reason. At least this didn't happen to you.

- Look on the bright side.

- Don't forget all the other good things in your life.

- That's not so bad. Let me share something similar that happened to me.

Highly Empathetic Replies

- I can't imagine what you are feeling, but I'm here for you.

- My heart aches for you and your family. How can I help?

- There are no words to say, but I'm hoping that with time, it becomes easier.

- You've worked hard and deserve the promotion. Congratulations.

- You are a warrior. I admire your bravery and strength. Man, you have endured so much.

- It means a lot that you would share this with me. It must be so difficult.

- Just know that you are not alone and are loved. I am here for you.

- I wish you didn't have to go through this and that I could take it all away.

- You are always there for others in need. Now, it's our turn to help you. I want to make this time easier for you. You are loved by many and need not go at this alone.

4 LEVERS TO ELEVATE YOUR EMPATHY

Lever #1: Ask Curious Questions

Do you recall your childhood when you had an inherent inquisitiveness that could not be quenched? You were fascinated with human behavior and the world around you, tirelessly asking curious questions. *What causes a double rainbow? Why does Grandpa breathe funny? Are we there yet? How many stars are in the galaxy?* Reignite your childlike curiosity as an adult. Curiosity fuels caring conversation and connection and makes life exponentially more intriguing.

Lever #2: Listen While Staying Present

Curiosity doesn't help if you aren't listening to the answers to your questions. We will delve into specific listening strategies later in the book, but for now, we all think we have better listening skills than we actually do, so be mindful of this shortfall. It's similar to how we think our driving skills are superior to what they actually are. Keep distractors, such as electronic devices, at bay; they vie for our attention and weaken our focus on others.

Lever #3: Express Concern for the Plights of Others

Try to understand a person's emotional state by imagining how you would feel if you or your loved ones experienced the same trial. Meet them where they are, not where you are. We all have a story, and we all want others to care about ours. How many times do people ask how you're doing and don't even stop long enough to listen to your answer? Show genuine interest in the personal lives of others, and not just those who can help you get ahead.

Actions speak louder than words when expressing empathy. Give a hug, check in, invite someone to coffee, or send a kind token of support and encouragement. And don't forget to congratulate others on their successes.

Lever #4: Open Up and Share

Transparency is alluring. People want to know the real, messy you. Be open about what matters to you and what may be getting in your way to achieve it. Be transparent about your areas for improvement. Showing vulnerability makes you more relatable and authentic, which draws others in. Share your worries, challenges, and dreams.

> 66
> Showing vulnerability makes you more relatable and authentic, which draws others in. Share your worries, challenges, and dreams.

A Personal Share: When my husband and I attended a networking event, we found ourselves in an awkward group conversation full of meaningless surface talk. Once I mentioned getting a new puppy because we were transitioning our children to *adulting*, my small share kickstarted a lively, substantive conversation rich with helpful advice, photos, and stories. Our transparent human connection led to new friendships.

The Power of Empathy Part 2

ELEVATE

Learn by Doing Exercises

1. Simulate an Empathetic Exchange

Ask a friend to have a conversation with you, then have them rate your empathy on a scale of one to five. As a conversation starter, launch a dialogue by having them share a tough trial they have endured. To help show your level of empathy, weave into the conversation the following four guiding principles:

a. **Ask curious questions.** Ask your conversation partner if there was any lesson learned that came from the trial or any purpose in their pain that added value to their life. Use their responses to prompt your additional questions of discovery.

b. **Keenly listen.** While conversing, prove that you are interested and listening well. Avoid taking mini mental vacations and stay laser-focused by using the proper amount of sustained eye contact. Your animation with interested facial expressions and gestures is key. Listen to understand; don't simply listen to reply. Asking several (not just one) curious questions about a point or story your conversation partner shared demonstrates that you've listened well enough to ask intelligent questions and that you care enough to learn more. This energizes others more than you can imagine.

c. **Express real concern.** Share how you wish they did not have to endure this, then indicate your admiration for their bravery and strength. Express your concern using one of the aforementioned Highly Empathetic Replies. Ask how you can help make things a little easier for them.

d. **Open up.** Share a relatable life experience that you or someone you know has endured. Show some vulnerability.

When the conversation concludes, ask your friend to rank you on the one to five Empathy Meter. How would they rank your ability to demonstrate genuine concern? If you fell short of a five, solicit feedback and keep practicing until you receive the ultimate high-five!

2. Make Empathy Your Own

Based on your experiences, share three taboo responses you've heard (or made yourself) that lack empathy:

a. _____

_____

b. _____

_____

c. _____

_____

Based on your experiences, share three empathetic responses that have provided comfort to you:

a. _____

_____

b. _____

_____

c. _____

_____

The Power of Building Relationship Capital

ENGAGE

Once upon a time,
unfortunate blunders were made . . .

Cora Wheelan was wildly underwhelmed with the notion that meaningful relationship-building was important to career success. After years of relentless bullying in school, the idea of Cora investing any more emotional sweat in winning popularity contests with the *cool adults* at her new company was preposterous. Been there, done that. Cozying up to coworkers, clients, or vendors was a waste of her time. Cora had earned a degree as a certified financial planner and was brilliant with her investment prowess on how to grow wealth. She had an uncanny sixth sense for pinpointing unique, tax-saving strategies that proved quite lucrative. When she relocated to be closer to her aging parents, she dreamed of starting a consulting business in this charming Southern town filled with friendly neighbors and Spanish moss dripping from stately oak trees. She envisioned Downton Abbey–like hospitality and history, long-lost chivalry, and a well-mannered society . . . a way of living that seemingly has passed us by.

Cora strategized a plan to differentiate herself as a savvy newcomer and earn the trust of this community. However, her competitor in the industry, Ned Bates, was born and raised in this town and offered very similar services. Winning people over proved far more difficult than she anticipated. She contacted a local radio station, offering to advise callers about their financial matters in exchange for exposure on the air. The station said it was only fair to offer the same opportunity to Ned to spark some friendly competition, which would benefit their listeners.

How did Cora, the newcomer, fare against her long-time resident competitor? Bridges were not only burnt but set aflame with fire and fury. You see, when a caller would consume an inordinate amount of time on the air picking Cora's brain about their financial predicament, Cora would routinely promise to contact them offline. The problem was that Cora neglected to keep her promises to follow up. Conversely, Ned spent as much time as needed on the air (and off) to serve the caller. Cora's reputation circled the drain and so did the prospect of a thriving business in the tight-knit small town.

Fast-forward a few months. The EVP of marketing for a nationally syndicated radio program was launching a major podcast. His goal was to recruit a small business owner who would serve as a subject matter expert and guest contributor to regularly appear on the podcast. Cora's name bubbled to the top of his radar. This exposure would have catapulted Cora's business to unprecedented heights.

However, this EVP did his homework and discovered that Cora had broken her promises to follow up with the radio show's listeners. However, his homework revealed that Ned was true to his word about following up. Who do you think the EVP rewarded for the courteous treatment of the listeners?

Moral of the story: As the saying goes, what goes around, comes around. Doing the right thing, especially when nobody is watching, paves the way for having the right thing done to you when everyone is watching.

ENLIGHTEN

with Ms. Tiffany's Epiphanies®

People do business with people they like and trust.

It may seem unfair, but likeability matters because it invites relatability and trust. Those who discount likeability and meaningful relationship-building will experience a startling wake-up call that they are not positioning themselves properly for advancement. Ultimately, one's relationship capital is the currency in business that promotes career success and personal fulfillment.

> " Ultimately, one's relationship capital is the currency in business that promotes career success and personal fulfillment.

DEFINE IT

Relationship capital is an alliance of trusted interconnections cultivated to enrich one's professional life with a strong support system. Oftentimes, personal friendships evolve from these professional bonds, which further enhances the closeness of the network.

WHILE WE'RE HERE

Building relationship capital remains a fluid, evolving journey that should be at the top of every to-do list if advancement is your goal. Your relationship reservoir needs to be consistently nurtured and pruned. Pruning your network improves the health of your relationship ecosystem. Pruning means to routinely assess who stays, who goes, and who needs to be closer. Snipping off the bad buds as you prune will allow your relationship capital to blossom with new life by keeping good company. Leaders need to surround themselves with positive, value-added contributors who attract other high-caliber influencers. Yes, technical skills are important. However, you can be the smartest person in the room, but if nobody relates to you or trusts you, your intellect is ignored.

In your quest to build relationship capital, devote energy toward meeting new people. When you're prospecting for these new acquaintances, seek people who don't look or think like you. The more diverse your relationship capital is, the more enrichment you will glean from the diversity of thought and experiences.

The 5-Step Approach to Boost Your Relationship Capital

1. **Create a Touchpoint Strategy.** When building your network, everyone is a potential candidate. Don't dismiss anyone as being irrelevant or unimportant. Every person has real value.

   - **Make a list of those with whom you wish to develop a closer relationship.** Hint: Familiarize yourself with your LinkedIn connections, noticing 1st- and 2nd-level connections and shared groups that you follow. Would you like to connect with one or more of these people?

- **Jot down your plan for reaching out to your targets.** Strike a healthy balance between virtual and in-person touchpoints. Are you going to grab coffee, or like/comment on or share their LinkedIn posts, or follow through with an unfulfilled favor? Keep track of your outreach, progress, and roadblocks.

- **Never burn a bridge.** A lasting impression has the potential to pack a greater punch than a first impression. Always gracefully exit situations you have outgrown. Wherever you go in life, always leave the situation with dignity and better than when you arrived. Just because you have moved on from an unfortunate experience doesn't mean you need to disparage those whose paths you have crossed. Ensure that your parting words don't burn any bridges and avoid any trash talking. An optimistic spirit is a differentiator that distinguishes you in today's world. At times, people mistakenly think of themselves as "realists," when they actually use this term as an excuse to be negative. Positivity is an infectious magnet that attracts other optimistic people, makes us more likeable, and elevates the caliber of our relationship capital. Each day, you get to choose your spirit: *Am I going to look for the good in people and find the good or look for the bad in people and find the bad?* What kind of person are YOU?

> "A positive thinker sees the invisible, feels the intangible, and achieves the impossible."
>
> —WINSTON CHURCHILL

2. **Audit Your Social Media Network.** You're only as good as the company you keep. If anyone brings toxicity to your network, reach for the pruning scissors to tidy your online network. For example, if you have a Cora Wheelan in your network, you can remove this person from your LinkedIn connections without them receiving a notification. Your network reflects you, and the company you keep is observed and judged.

3. **Don't Forget the *Forgotten Network*.** When expanding your network, consider rekindling dormant relationships from your past that used to be stronger. These ties push you outside of your comfy inner circle that may not be sparking fresh ideas or generating value-added contacts. David Burkus, author of *Friend of a Friend*,[6] said it wisely:

> "Much of the conventional networking advice is focused on . . . meeting brand-new people. While that is a noble goal . . . reactivating old connections is much faster than building a brand-new relationship from scratch."

---

[6] David Burkus, *Friend of a Friend: Understanding the Hidden Networks That Can Transform Your Life and Your Career* (New York: Houghton Mifflin Harcourt Publishing Company, 2018).

4. **Help Others.** Shift your perspective toward how you can help others instead of thinking *me, me, me.* Instead of asking how you can get ahead, ask how you can be a value-added contributor to your employer. Instead of thinking your employer just keeps heaping on the workload without paying additional compensation, maintain an others-focused, healthier attitude. You'll discover that you will eventually be viewed as a dedicated team player and will reap unexpected dividends down the road. You will enjoy professional rewards, and most importantly, enjoy the personal fulfillment of paying value forward. Remember, what goes around comes around. As Winston Churchill counseled, "We make a living by what we get, but we make a life by what we give."

5. **Create a Dependable Inner Circle of Trust.**
A Personal Share: My family teases me that when I embrace a new product or service provider, exercise routine, adventure, book, recipe, song, Netflix show, etc., it must be because a member of my *circle of trust* recommended it. Guilty as charged! Once a person makes their way into my personal circle of trust, their opinion is highly regarded, and that person can do no wrong in my eyes. The same premise can be applied to your professional network. Create a professional circle of trust composed of experts who offer guidance on financial, legal, and industry subject matter, as well as community service. It could be a formal advisory board, mentor, or individual go-to expert who holds you accountable and stands ready to support, or simply a trusted person who has your back.

Grow Your Network

ELEVATE

Learn by Doing Exercises

SOMETHING OLD, NEW, BORROWED, AND BLUE. ARE YOU READY TO SAY "I DO"?

This wedding tradition is a fun way to remember how to marry your past with your present so your future is brighter with robust relationship capital.

- **Something Old.** Create a target list of dormant relationships from your past and a plan of actionable steps to reconnect with these long-lost friends. Your list could include high school or college friends with whom you've lost touch. Research their career path on LinkedIn, send them an invite, and start a conversation online. Reconnect in person after you have earned their trust online.

- **Something New.** Make it a goal each week to schedule at least two networking coffees with new acquaintances.

Search for a commonality between the two of you for bonding purposes. Ask these questions: *How can I help you achieve your goals? What can I do to add value to your life?*

- **Something Borrowed.** Borrow the assistance of your network. Request introductions to their friends who would appreciate exploring synergies between your business and theirs. You'll find that people love to help and feel valued when they do.

- **Something Blue.** Don't be blue and take it personally if your request to network is dismissed. Busy schedules and different priorities prevail. Remember: If you don't ask, you won't get.

Brilliant Conversation and Keen Listening

Turning Difficult Conversations into Civil Discourse

ENGAGE

Once upon a time,
unfortunate blunders were made . . .

There once were a brother and sister who were not only twins but also the best of friends. They were bonded together so closely that they could practically finish each other's sentences. One day while texting, they became engaged in a divisive political exchange. Things got heated.

Brother:

Hey sis, what's new? Did the family vote?

Sister:

Hi bud, I've had better days. Yes, my kids are early voting. I just wish they would vote differently. Oh well, not much I can do about it.

Brother:

Whoa! You mean to tell me that your kids aren't voting for our guy?

Sister:

It is what it is. I'm suffering from political drama fatigue and tired of worrying about it.

Brother:

Unbelievable. Thought they were more intelligent.

Sister:

They *are* intelligent but feel differently than we do. That's what makes a democracy.

Brother:

Tell my nephew and niece that they need to think for themselves and not just vote how their friends and social media pressure them to vote.

Sister:

My children are strong, independent thinkers, and as long as they are making informed decisions, I respect their right to vote how they choose.

Brother:

We'll agree to disagree, kiddo. You know they would be schooled differently if I ever talked politics with them. I thought you raised them better.

3 Days Later

Brother:

Hey sis, my bad. Really sorry about my harsh comments about the kids and you.

Sister:

I appreciate your apology. I went to bed sad thinking I'd lost my best friend.

ENLIGHTEN

with Ms. Tiffany's Epiphanies®

3 TECHNIQUES TO TURN DIFFICULT CONVERSATIONS INTO CIVIL DISCOURSE

Is talking politics worth the risk of alienating a colleague, client, friend, or family member? Or in today's cancel culture, should we keep striving to "agree to disagree" so our points are heard and not cancelled? Our society is bearing witness to an unprecedented, scary phenomenon that stands to weaken our relationships and move us into a contentious future that will need to be reckoned with if we stay the course. Why has it become increasingly rare for people to agree to disagree—especially today, when tolerance and open-mindedness are often touted as essential in a modern-day culture of progress?

I often wonder, *Wait, let me get this correct—if your opinion doesn't mirror mine, I am irrational and wrong, and you are the enlightened one?* Alarmingly, political discourse has become as volatile as gunpowder, triggering fractured relationships in a polarized country.

How we respond when we feel challenged is the key to unlocking civil discourse. Modern business etiquette is about exhibiting heightened self-awareness and disciplined restraint with the goal of employing our highest-caliber communication skills for meaningful relationship-building and authentic leadership.

> **Modern business etiquette is about exhibiting heightened self-awareness and disciplined restraint with the goal of employing our highest-caliber communication skills for meaningful relationship-building and authentic leadership.**

At the close of every business day, relationship-building is the most important component for business success in any industry.

> **Let's rescue contentious conversations from sharp barbs and seething resentment by honing our tools of persuasion.**

Let's rescue contentious conversations from sharp barbs and seething resentment by honing our tools of persuasion. Simply put, let's lengthen our fuses and enrich our minds by patiently listening.

Albert Einstein cautioned, "Once you stop learning, you start dying." Try learning something from another generation or (*gasp!*) from across the political party aisle. Finding that sweet spot between expressing your individualism and caring enough to learn from the opinions of others portrays intelligence, discernment, maturity, and business acumen.

Use the 3-point framework of Expression, Repression, and Inquisition the next time you want to engage in civil discourse to avoid unhealthy conflict.

1. Expression

Expressing yourself with dignity and decorum means listening with an open mind and employing high-caliber communication skills. Be mindful not to dominate the conversation or base your argument on an abundance of one-sided research that validates your biased view. Inevitably, there's always counter research available at your audience's fingertips. If you find you are talking more, pause and solicit their opinion. Emphasize that you are interested in learning from their perspective. When trying to convince someone of your point, it's highly effective to use a personal example that relates to your counterpart's life. This will instantly pique their attention and perk their hearing. Be careful not to interrupt or talk over your counterpart. Remember that interruption or finishing someone's sentence for them breaks down trust and are signs of undeveloped people skills. If all else fails, know that you can nearly always relieve the pressure in a conversation with three magical words: *Tell me more.*

2. Repression

Often, we shut down when someone disagrees with us. We resort to dismissive body language such as quick half-gestures as if to wave their point away, resolving not to broach the subject again. It's a shame to feel constricted in expressing our individualism. This leads to weakened relationships and resentment that could boil over at the slightest provocation. It also dumbs down communication since we tend to stick with the safer, surface-level small talk. When an outburst starts bubbling up inside, strive to be less reactive. Step back and employ self-restraint. Think before you speak about how you can respond in a more skillful way, incorporating keen listening and empathic understanding. Warren Buffett stated, "True power is restraint. If words control you, that means everyone else can control you. Breathe and allow things to pass."

Speaking of breathing, when you're tempted to interrupt, repeat this phrase in your mind: *Hard stop; don't interrupt.* As you're listening, push out all the air in your lungs, inhale through your nose for several seconds, hold, then exhale from your mouth, slowly so as to maintain your inner and outer equipoise (don't give the impression you are a bull preparing to charge). Find a place of calm and savor a composed state.

3. Inquisition

Return to that state of childlike wonder and demonstrate curiosity about the reasons others disagree. Say, "We may have differing views, but I'm always interested in widening my understanding. Tell me more." Ask clarifying questions to subtly reveal your perspective: "Are you concerned about how this candidate's tax increase may impact your family? I'm worried about its ramifications for my business."

By employing this framework, we are more apt to walk away from these conversations reassured that we've respectfully demonstrated that the other person's opinions mattered yet still expressed our individualism. Let's breathe, soften our tone, expand our capacity to change our minds, and avoid the urge to shut down and ghost that relationship. Ghosting another human solves nothing and brings out the worst in all.

ELEVATE

Learn by Doing Exercises

1. Turn Back Time

Now that you have these tools in your toolbelt, recall a debate that you witnessed or actively engaged in that unraveled into an unfortunate ending. Write a new version incorporating the 3-point framework of Expression, Repression, and Inquisition so your rewritten story has a happier ending. Practice these new strategies in future conversations.

2. Change the Outcome

Time to switch roles! Now you are the author, not the reader. Visualize someone in your life who has vehemently disagreed with you. Write a story about you two disagreeing on a topic that has led to arguments in the past. Use the 3-point framework to reimagine and rewrite the outcome.

Curiosity—Your Gateway to Engagement

ENGAGE

Once upon a time,
unfortunate blunders were made . . .

Blunder 1: If only I had asked curious questions to elevate my leadership visibility.

New hire Savannah Newbie was ablaze with excitement at the prospect of meeting the CEO at the monthly *Lunch with the Leader*. When the CEO arrived early to the luncheon, Savannah was the only one present. Moments before her arrival, the CEO had accepted a new role, which she briefly described to Savannah. It turns out the CEO was leading a major citywide fundraising campaign for a high-profile arts organization. It was a high-risk, high-reward endeavor that had presented itself at a challenging time for the CEO, as her business was in the midst of launching a series of new product lines.

Though Savannah noticed that the CEO seemed a bit preoccupied, she didn't let that stop her from seizing the moment to strategically introduce herself before launching into a litany of feelings about her new job. Abruptly, the CEO apologized and excused herself to take a call.

Savannah's lack of inquisitiveness about the CEO's circumstances didn't win her any favors. Imagine the favorable impression Savannah could have burned into the memory of this key stakeholder had she, instead, steered the conversation toward helping the CEO with curious questions like:

- I would be honored to help you in any way with this important initiative. What committees do you envision assembling to execute your campaign work?

- Do you have individuals in mind to lead these committees?

- Oh, you have a Women's Roundtable? I used to own a business focused on women's empowerment. Are you interested in new hires pitching in to help you with your campaign?

Savannah missed an *"opportunity wink"* that could have propelled her career. Stay others-focused and ask curious questions to unearth ways to add significant value to their lives.

Blunder 2: If only I had asked curious questions to boost my team's morale.

It was the week before the global pandemic erupted and all was right with the world, especially for Mitch Manger. He received the good news that his aviation industry company had promoted him to sales manager. Unfortunately, he had limited time to meet his sales team of thirty-five employees before they were ordered to quarantine at home and work remotely for months.

Each week, Mitch led a virtual team huddle, along with one-on-one meetings. Much to the team's dismay, the touch-base meetings were not interactive. Mitch assumed the role of a lecturing talking head, harping on how the team was under-performing and needed to sell, sell, and sell more. There was no discussion about how the employees were handling the transition to the new normal of isolation. Mitch never covered what the employer could do to make achieving a work-life balance easier in light of the new set of challenges. Virtual fatigue became an everyday obstacle to productivity, though Mitch never expressed any empathy or imparted any coping strategies. Morale plummeted, and year-end numbers bleakly reflected Mitch's *head-in-the-sand* management approach.

If only Mitch would have asked curious questions like:

- How are you personally dealing with working from home? Are you having to homeschool the kids? How is the health of your family? Do you have any high-risk family members that you may need some flexibility to help?

- As your manager, how can I help you succeed? How often would you like to connect and what time of day is most convenient for you?

- Are there any goals that seem daunting or unrealistic to you? Do you need help from the interns or other resources we have available?

ENLIGHTEN

with Ms. Tiffany's Epiphanies®

Hello, my name is Curiosity, not to be confused
with my bored brother, Disinterested. We have not yet had
the pleasure of meeting. I go by George, but nobody
monkeys around with me. I should be your BFF for
the sake of advancement, reminding you to return to a
childlike state of wonder. Alas, I often get forgotten.
I'm the question mark that energizes and amplifies like
a shot of caffeine, adding gusto to life. I am the rare exertion
of effort made by few, the difference between caring less
about hearing yourself talk and more about what others have
to say. I am the trait that fosters connection and trust.
When I help, instead of ruling by dictatorship, you
inspire talent. Once we grow tighter, you become interesting,
but more importantly, interested. Stick with me, and I will
strengthen your network. I am the disrupter to a one-dimensional
point of view. I am the standing invite to an intellectually
stimulating conversation. I am the Wizard of Oz when
the filming transitions from black and white to color.
Dare not be lulled into foolish belief that asking questions
reveals ignorance or weakness. On the contrary,
it underscores brilliance. Dare not undervalue me.
I matter in making your world more intriguing.

THE FORGOTTEN SKILL

Curiosity is wildly overlooked as one of the most valuable professional development tools for tightly securing a competitive advantage. The practice of curiosity is the conscious choice to act on a desire to learn new things. If you are ambitious, becoming a lifelong learner is a smart choice. Lifelong learners pursue wisdom, experience, and captivating stories by viewing life through a curious lens no matter how advanced they are in their career. This curiosity invites you to develop a deeper humility. When you have an insatiable curiosity about people, you align yourself with an elite group of influencers who are equipped with powerful connections to share.

THE SUPERPOWER OF CURIOSITY

When you converse, resist the all-too-common urge to stop after only asking one or two questions. Provocatively probe by asking curious questions until your conversations reveal surprise and intrigue. Base your next question on your counterpart's previous sentences, not on the preplanned agenda in your head pressing to be heard.

> Provocatively probe by asking curious questions until your conversations reveal surprise and intrigue. Base your next question on your counterpart's previous sentences, not on the preplanned agenda in your head pressing to be heard.

A Personal Share: Recently, I shared my excitement about becoming an author with another business leader. He asked one question: "What's the name of your book?" That was it. He didn't ask how it was being published, who the target audience was, what inspired me, what my marketing plans were, who my publisher was, and the list goes on. He missed his shot to engage and deepen our relationship. I left the conversation with little interest in sharing something personal with him again.

Conversely, I shared the same news about becoming a new author with two of my clients. I was struck with how dramatically their responses differed. The first client grabbed my attention, excitedly replying, "Congratulations, Tiffany! How can our company help you promote the book and make it successful in the marketplace?" She then asked another curious question that demonstrated her interest and energized me. "Knowing what you know now, would you write another book in the future or is this a one-and-done project?"

The second client thoughtfully inquired, "I'm curious—now that you have completed your manuscript, is it like an old friend who moved away and you don't get to see anymore? Are there days when you miss getting in the zone and writing, or is it a relief to have the writing grind behind you?"

Wow, do you see the power of curiosity? It has a rippling effect and is the fork in the road presenting two paths—one that deepens relationships and one that weakens or alienates relationships. Which path do you want to walk in your career?

If you walk away from a conversation rolling your eyes at how boring it was, you likely didn't ask curious questions—and that's on you. I often advised my sons growing up that if they were bored, that means they are boring people, and they are certainly not boring. Therefore, my message was for them to try harder to create a more interesting day. That advice applies to having intriguing conversattions as well.

HOW DOES CURIOSITY SECURE A COMPETITIVE ADVANTAGE?

1. Curiosity sets you apart with rare professional courtesy and concern for others.

2. Curiosity elevates empathy and instills authenticity.

3. Curiosity inspires an *others-focused* mentality, where you learn about the needs of others so you are better positioned to add value to their lives.

4. Curiosity equips the introvert with an easy task of asking questions in order to project confidence. Even if you have a reserved personality and are not likely to offer up a witty quip or engaging story, you're more capable of winning people over than you think—anyone can ask questions!

5. Curiosity deepens relationships and earns trust. It also serves as a boomerang back to you beneficially; your counterpart will keep returning for engagement since they are more comfortable with you now and have been amplified in energy.

6. Curiosity serves as a smooth icebreaker to relieve awkwardness and inhibitions between people not knowing what to say in conversations. When you wittily start a conversation by asking a curious question that energizes, you are viewed as a savvy conversationalist. At the end of this chapter, I'll

provide some specific examples of impressive conversation starters that are sure to wow and impress.

Case in Point: A Curious New Practice at the New Practice

A Personal Share: I went to my dentist's office for a routine cleaning. I wasn't expecting anything but to exchange pleasantries and leave with a clean mouth, but I was happily mistaken. Don't you love when life throws you a curve ball and your day becomes brighter because of it? It turned out that my long-time dentist had retired, and a new dentist had acquired his practice. What in the world did that dental staff do to make such a favorable impression? They were curious.

When I sat down in the dental chair, feeling sharp-pointed instruments poking and prodding along my gum line, the hygienist started to chat. "How is your older son in Chicago doing after having to postpone his wedding due to the pandemic?" she asked.

"Wow, you have a good memory!" I responded. She smiled and explained the hygienists started maintaining personal notes in patients' charts so the staff would remember to ask curious questions.

When the doctor entered the room to give his stamp of approval of the cleaning, he asked, "How's the manuscript writing going for the new book?" I was floored. Although I understood that this was a new procedure implemented at the office and not spontaneous expressions of interest, I still felt they cared enough to make notes and seemed to have genuine interest in my responses. I left feeling valued and buoyant in spirit. How driven are you to leave others feeling buoyant in spirit after having a conversation with you?

ELEVATE

Learn by Doing Exercise

THE CURIOSITY CREED

Post on your mirror and each morning recite the Curiosity Creed.

C   I promise to ask **captivating** questions so that others feel valued and energized.

U   I promise to enhance my **understanding** of other perspectives through empathy and build a reservoir to draw from of knowledge and experiences.

R   I promise to **remember** key details from curious conversations and follow up about these details in subsequent conversations.

I   I promise to be more **interested** rather than **interesting**.

O   I promise to be vulnerable and **open** up about myself to discover commonalities and inspire transparency in others.

U   I promise to **undo** my poor habit of listening to reply instead of listening to understand.

S   I promise to ask questions until a **surprise** or element of intrigue is revealed.

Keen Listening—
The North Star of a Great Leader

ENGAGE

> "When I listen,
> I have the power
> ... When I talk,
> I give it away."

Once upon a time,
unfortunate blunders were made ...

—VOLTAIRE, PHILOSOPHER

Listening is far more than just politely waiting for your turn to speak. Keen listening takes an abundance of patience and is about discovering, validating, and amplifying others to achieve deeper connections.

How Do Keen Listening Skills Impact Upward Mobility in Your Career?

We are suffering collectively from a figurative chronic hearing loss in our society. We simply don't listen. Oftentimes, the key to career advancement is not about what you say but more about how proficient you are in intently listening. This is a common complaint from today's upper echelon about their organizational members in today's world and vice versa. When we do listen, it's often selective and contingent on receiving what we hope to hear. If we don't like what's being recited, we tend to shut down and take mini mental vacations to distant tropical islands.

If we aren't present and engaged in the moment, we are focusing more on ourselves than on others. This myopic thinking can stunt our career growth by fostering shallow relationships.

A Leader's North Star: Perfecting Our Listening Skills

Great leaders must be strong communicators, possessing the powers of persuasion and motivation. Many mistakenly believe that strong communication is reserved only for writing or public speaking. However, an even greater communication talent is foolishly undervalued: the skill of keen listening.

Senior management also needs to take caution: A gradual hearing loss can slowly manifest itself as one climbs the corporate ladder. Listening may become a greater challenge for fast trackers because their success may lull them into being more interested in talking *at* their employees instead of *with* them. Andy Stanley brilliantly surmised, "Leaders who don't listen will eventually be surrounded by people who have nothing to say." On the other hand, when organizational members feel heard and validated, they respond with a fierce loyalty. The ultimate, most genuine way of showing respect is to keenly listen.

A PRESIDENTIAL RASCAL

U.S. President Franklin D. Roosevelt's nickname was *Houdini in the White House*. But even with a magician's title, he couldn't make the agonizingly long receiving lines at the White House disappear. He detested these lines, lamenting that no one listened to what he said. So FDR thought of a clever plan marked by his signature wit. When he next extended his hand in the receiving line, he remarked, "I murdered my grandmother this morning," just to see who was listening. Most guests replied, "Excellent! Good work and God bless you!" One day, the Bolivian ambassador quipped, "I am sure she had it coming." Just goes to show that acute listening skills are always essential!

When lively and fun communication is employed, trusted relationships form organically and effortlessly. These relationships are every great leader's North Star because they make for a powerful network interconnected with trusted advisors, loyal talent, supporters, and accountability partners. Simply put, trusted relationships bring out the best in us, both professionally and socially.

with Ms. Tiffany's Epiphanies®

Hello, my name is Listen, not to be confused
with my chatty sis, Overshare. Of course, we've met,
but quite frankly, you haven't been all ears.
I am the mindfulness that nudges you to stay present and
be insatiably curious. I represent the sincerest form of
how you show respect to others. I am the reminder to
pull the cotton from your ears and realize why we have
two ears yet only one mouth. Once we grow closer,
you'll ask intelligent questions at just the right moment.
When that moment arrives, I am there to spark chemistry
and charisma. I am the reason you are undistracted
at a noisy event. I am the bridge to cross over for
all who know you to feel buoyant in spirited communication.
Dare not be lulled into foolish belief that I do not have a job.
My job is to amplify and embolden by listening patiently
and not passively. Honor me each day, and I become
music to the ears of all whom you meet . . .
a symphony that harmonizes in quiet sound.

7 ROADBLOCKS TO EMPATHETIC LISTENING

Doors of opportunity swing wide open once our self-awareness is heightened to these seven roadblocks to active listening:

1. Illusion of Superiority

In the same way that many people believe their driving or cooking skills are better than most, we allow ourselves to slip into a delusional state of mind when we assume that our listening skills are exceptional. Our state of denial has a lasting impact on our ability to engage, amplify, and build trust.

2. Distractions and Daydreaming

Our world is noisy, with two types of distractions vying for our attention: psychological and physical. When we are conversing, we often transgress into autopilot, drifting into a mind-numbing fog of wandering. If we don't follow what people say, we aren't equipped to ask intellectually stimulating questions, and our counterpart is likely to feel unheard.

Physical distractions such as an email ping, a "like" on social media, a text notification on your watch, or an influential person walking into the room can wreak havoc on maintaining a sustained attention span. Be intentio nal with your focus. Create a perception with your conversational counterpart that they are the only person who matters in that moment.

3. Ease of Recording

Technology is both a blessing and a curse. In today's world of smartphones, instead of listening we pull out our devices to record audio or video. These convenient recordings provide an excuse to zone out in the moment, thinking we'll pay attention to the recording later. We miss out on taking a mental snapshot in real life that is cherished long after the image gets lost in our phone's gallery.

4. The Loss of Empathy

Empathy, as noted previously, is plummeting in today's world. While disheartening, this presents a golden opportunity for you to set yourself apart. There is a dire need for authentic listeners, those who are empathetic to the opinions and plights of others, regardless of whether or not they agree with those opinions. Dianne Crampton said it well: "Empathy is a universal team value that promotes high commitment and cooperation in the workplace."[7]

5. Discomfort with Silence

There is power in the pause. Resist the urge to fill gaps of silence in a conversation. As Abraham Lincoln wisely quipped, "It's better to remain silent and be thought a fool than to speak out and remove all doubt."

"It's better to remain silent and be thought a fool than to speak out and remove all doubt."

— ABRAHAM LINCOLN

6. Listening to Reply, Not Listening to Understand

Are you listening to a person only to critically judge them? Are you listening to poke holes in their reasoning? Communication problems occur because we often don't listen to understand and to find

---

[7] Dianne Crampton, "Empathy: Why It Is Important," April 18, 2011, https://corevalues.com/culture/team-cultures/empathy-why-it-is-important/.

the good in what's being said. Instead, we listen to reply. To be others-focused, resist the temptation to plan your next words and base your response on your counterpart's prior two to three sentences. People who find themselves struggling with an insatiable urge to debate when listening should remember the three Cs to dead-end conversations: criticism, competitiveness, and combativeness.

7. Absence of Nonverbal Encouragement and Validation

When you listen, are you aware of what your facial expressions and voice are doing? Are you exhibiting engaged eye contact, a stimulated eyebrow flash, and the occasional nodding of your head in agreement? Are you expressing surprise or agreement verbally? Nonverbal communication speaks the loudest. Humans open up more when they see the affirmation these nonverbal cues provide because they believe you are keenly interested and championing their ideas. Acute listeners entice and enhance interactions, which promotes likeability and trust.

ELEVATE

Learn by Doing Exercises

1. **Unscramble and Reassemble:** Many people believe there are no coincidences in life. Here's a case in point in which two words are justifiably spelled with the same letters. Unscramble the word shown below and use all the letters to make a new word. The new word should correlate directly to what we are learning in this section. Can you take a guess?

S. ЛЛ T.

2. **Polish Your Listening Prowess**: In order to strengthen our muscles of staying present in the moment to keenly listen, practice this exercise. The next time you find yourself in a noisy setting, improve your listening prowess by identifying each sound present in the room individually—background conversations, silverware clanging, birds singing, an air conditioner turning on. Create a visual in your mind of taking each sound you identify and placing it on a shelf with each sound in its own labeled box. You'll soon have a sharpened skill of listening more intently.

If you rearrange the letters in SILENT, you can spell LISTEN, and it's not by coincidence that these two words are cleverly interrelated.

Captivating Conversation Starters

ELEVATE

Learn by Doing Exercises

Conversation Starters: Jump-start any dull dialogue with these curious questions:

- Do you remember your first concert?

- What is the most selfish thing you've done and what is your proudest moment?

- What are three unique apps on your phone and why are they there?

- What are your last three shareable photos on your phone?

- If you had your choice of a last meal on earth, who would cook it and what would it be?

- If you could invite three people you don't know but admire (dead or alive) to dinner, who would they be and what curious question would you ask them?

- What do you care about most other than your family?

- If your childhood had a scent, what would it be? (For example: fresh-cut grass, freshly baked cinnamon rolls, tobacco leaves hanging in a barn, pipe or cigarette smoke, burnt cooking, apple pie, etc.)

- If your house was burning and your family was safe, what would you grab before running out the door other than your phone?

- As you awake from a six-month coma, what show would you binge-watch first? What TikTok dance would you want to practice first?

- What is the most valuable piece of unexpected advice you've received?

- What movie could you watch a million times?

Look for opportunities to ask these conversation starters in real life so you'll become adept at launching lively conversations.

1. Name your 3 favorite curious questions from above, write them here, and commit them to memory.

_____

_____

_____

2. Over the next few weeks, ask others your favorite curious questions and jot down what additional curious questions you posed as the dialogue flowed. Keep working to expand your repertoire of curious questions.

_____

_____

_____

3. Name three additional interesting conversation starters of your own.

_____

_____

_____

Working a Room with a Plan and Networking for Results

Steer Clear of
5 Networking Blunders

ENGAGE

Once upon a time,
unfortunate blunders were made . . .

"You can have everything in life you want if you
will just help enough people get what they want."

— ZIG ZIGLAR

Networking Blunder #1: The Dread of Networking Events

I Am Only Talking to My Dog Today

My name is Nellie, and I am not the cheeriest person on the
planet. As an engineer, I have the prowess of a NASA genius with

analytical, critical thinking, and problem-solving skills that are simply unmatched. What doesn't come so naturally to me is interacting with other people. Simply put, it pains me beyond measure to talk to anyone except my dog.

I was recently awarded a coveted promotion to lead an elite team. However, since it requires intense networking and hobnobbing with high-profile snoozers in hopes of securing funding resources for my team, I'm not thrilled. Have I mentioned that I would rather be home watching Netflix with my dog than attending a networking event?

Nellie's Blunder

Negative Nellie's pessimistic vibe is a deterrent to likeability and is sure to repel people at events. Ironically, her sharp wit could make her a refreshingly intriguing conversationalist if she would just brighten her disposition with a more positive mindset. Nellie naively assumes that she will roll in late to networking events, briskly meet the influencers, spew her wish list of wants, and saunter away with a windfall of pledges for her team.

Networking Blunder #2: Waiting to Network Until You Need to

Jerry is a recovering procrastinator who is convinced that waiting to complete a task, big or small, activates a surge of adrenaline necessary to best execute tasks. To illustrate, at law school Jerry had a comprehensive final exam in contract law. On the day before this daunting endeavor, he started searching for his class folder containing past exams and crucial notes. Jerry experienced quite the rude awakening when it dawned on him that he had unknowingly lost this class folder chock-full of critical curriculum. If only he hadn't waited until the last minute to get his act in gear!

Once he graduated law school and became a new hire at a firm, the hiring partner laid out Jerry's career track. Jerry pondered when it would be wise to start networking efforts to position himself to achieve his new business development goals. Networking would become essential in generating leads, prospects, and new clients and meeting centers of influence who would make referrals to Jerry. As a junior associate, the firm wasn't ready for him to act in a sales/client-facing role—he first needed to gain experience practicing law and supporting senior attorneys. However, according to the firm's career track, this expectation would trigger at the six-year mark, the earliest he could make partner.

As Jerry pondered all this, he remained true to his procrastination habit. Below is the firm's career track and Jerry's beliefs about when he should begin his networking efforts:

- **Year 0–2:** New hire—No business development goals required (yet).

- **Year 3–5:** Associate—No business goals required (yet).

- **Year 6–10:** Partner—Now! Business development begins.

Wake Up and Smell the Coffee

In Jerry's world of delusion, he was under the impression that he had plenty of time to start networking since his new business goals were not due to be met for another six years. Rise and shine, Jerry! Placing networking efforts on the back burner isn't a smart chess move. The chess prodigy in *The Queen's Gambit* would be sorely disappointed with the poor planning. After all, today's planning is a glide path to tomorrow's achievements.

Networking Blunder #3: Beware of the 3 Bs—Bar, Buffet, and Buddies

Former General Electric CEO Jack Welch used networking events such as cocktail parties to vet his early career professionals and learn who was serious about positioning themselves for upward mobility. Would they rise to the occasion of working the room with a plan or would they just head to the bar, buffet, and their buddies for a good time?

> Your employer doesn't invite you to networking events because they're worried about you being thirsty, hungry, or lonely.

Raising Your Bar

An invitation to a networking event is a gift from your employer to you and should be viewed as an essential job requirement not to be missed or dismissed just because it lands at the end of a tiring day. If it's an internal occasion, enjoy the opportunity to be noticed and positively evaluated. For client-facing events, your employer has thought long and hard about who to send to these paid sponsored events to represent the company as their ambassador to the public.

Your employer doesn't do this because they're worried about you being thirsty, hungry, or lonely. They invite you to develop relationships in pursuit of the organization's goals, which inevitably positions you for success. The average worker often is a no-show—or they'll merely attend long enough to check the box of being seen. When you take these networking events seriously and show up, you differentiate yourself with excellence by being a proud ambassador for your employer.

Networking Blunder #4: The Myth—Introverts Are Lousy Networkers

Who would earn your trust more at a networking event?

The Extrovert: Remember Bentley Fosset from Building Block 1, Week 1? How could we forget! He was the hotshot who thought he was God's gift to the world. A wide-eyed, eager Ivy League graduate who was newly hired by a global data analytic enterprise, Bentley was raring to set the world on fire and make his indelible mark on society. In his high school and college years, he was smooth as glass, dazzling his teachers and community with his sparkling charisma and razor-sharp wit. Everything in life seemed to come effortlessly for him, and he savored success at every turn. This experience caused him to expect that rapid advancement would come easily and early in his career. However, Bentley's inflated ego caused him to fail at a key skill for rapid advancement: winning people over in the business world. Life changes when we start *adulting* in the real world.

The Introvert: Remember David Drier from Building Block 2, Week 1? David was humble and likeable, answering each interview question thoughtfully while sharing engaging stories that validated his track record and pulled at the interviewer's heartstrings. When the HR director pointed out that David's leg had been shaking nonstop, David blushed and quipped that he was guilty as charged and was working to eliminate this nervous tic. He grinned earnestly, thanking the director for her candor. Unsurprisingly, David was awarded the job because of his likeability, not to mention coachability. The director was drawn to his charming self-deprecation when he showed grace under pressure.

Networking Blunder #5: Poor Business Card Exchanges

The manner by which you present, receive, and stow your business cards at a networking event or during any initial interaction says a lot about your polish, professionalism, and business acumen. The timing with which you exchange business cards is also paramount. Some people prematurely hand their card out in a less-than-professional way before any relationship has begun to blossom or any trust is kindled. Avoid the temptation to indiscriminately hand out your cards as though you're handing out flyers at a hardware store's grand opening. Timing is key in business. Your card will be better received and taken more seriously if you know when and how to exchange using proper business card protocol.

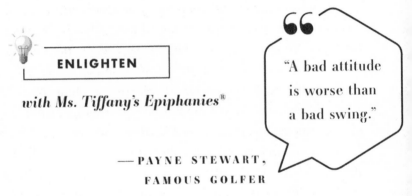

ENLIGHTEN

with Ms. Tiffany's Epiphanies®

"A bad attitude is worse than a bad swing."

— PAYNE STEWART, FAMOUS GOLFER

Overcome Networking Blunder #1: The Dread of Networking Events

It's painfully obvious when someone dreads a networking event, no matter what kind of poker face is presented. To avoid a swing and a miss at networking events, heighten your self-awareness of Nellie's likely shortfalls:

- Exuding negativity, which depletes energy and joy from others

- Being distracted by her phone

- Complaining to the waitstaff

- Arriving late with a frown and crossed arms

- Adopting an air of superiority and boredom

- Jumping straight to her business agenda, instead of connecting on a personal level

Fake It 'Til You Make It

Your entrance at a networking event is observed more than you know. If you arrive with a frown and furrowed brow, chances are you won't appear approachable. Your body language instead must exude positivity and friendliness. Notify your face that you're happy to be there (even if you're not) with a soft smile seconds before entering. Activating an eye sparkle brightens the face as well. Soon networking will feel natural and fun because your open body posture and facial expression will help you relax and engage in easygoing conversations that lead to new opportunities.

> "Seven days without laughter makes one weak!"
>
> —*BEETLE BAILEY*, COMIC STRIP CHARACTER

Your Smile: The Overlooked Welcome Sign

Smiling is contagious and projects cheerfulness, buoyancy, and warmth. Smiling also releases feel-good endorphins that help settle your nerves. Think of your smile as a welcome sign that signals you are a happy person whom people want to get to know.

Remember to maintain sustained, undistracted eye contact and to carry yourself with confidence in an upright, non-slouching posture with your arms at home base (by your sides), not in pockets, clasped in the insecure fig-leaf position, or hiding behind your back.

Overcome Networking Blunder #2: Waiting to Network Until You Need to

Are you a planner? You should be if you want to advance in your career. If you keep the long game in mind, you'll need to start networking sooner rather than later. As Gary Player, retired South African professional golfer, stated, "The harder you practice, the luckier you get."

Let's revisit the career track of Jerry the procrastinator:

- **Year 0–2:** New hire—No business development goals required (yet).

- **Year 3–5:** Associate—No business goals required (yet).

- **Year 6–10:** Partner—Now! Business development begins.

> People will take your call after you have built a trusting relationship and before you need something.

Jerry doesn't need to worry about generating new clients and prospects for another six years, so why begin networking now?

Jerry needs to start reaching out *now* as a junior associate. He needs to be vigilant at scheduling weekly networking coffees or monthly leadership touch-bases to form internal alliances that will lead to external referrals. Attending numerous networking events, leveraging LinkedIn to stay on people's radar, and expanding his networking circle now will reap long-term dividends when it counts the most.

Overcome Networking Blunder #3: Beware of the 3 Bs— Bar, Buffet, and Buddies

Before succeeding at any networking event, goal setting is paramount. Set realistic, yet aggressive goals for those with whom you want to connect at each event before indulging in the 3 Bs. Familiarize yourself with the attendee roster, which will require planning ahead and committing to doing your pre-event homework. Be mindful of these points when establishing your personal goals for whom to meet at a networking event:

- **Visualize Your Victory.** What does your approach look like for each person? What questions will you have prepared? How realistic and achievable are your goals? Imagine yourself walking out the door after having a productive night of networking, feeling confident that you have made meaningful connections.

- **Follow Up.** Promptly plan actionable steps that you'll take in the days following an event when you contact your new acquaintances. Keep the steps simple and genuine.

- **Grant Yourself Grace.** If a conversation doesn't go smoothly, don't take it personally and be hard on yourself. Perhaps the other person had a bad day or something else is going on in their life that's unrelated to you. Simply reappraise what may have gone wrong to tweak your approach.

- **Persevere with Patience.** Be flexible with your timeline and goals. Trust that as long as you consistently appear and engage at events, your networking circle will prosper, and you may even enjoy some surprise encounters that lead to fruitful lifelong friendships.

Overcome Networking Blunder #4: The Myth—Introverts Are Lousy Networkers

Bentley or David? With whom would I be more interested in spending time at a networking event? Definitely David, the introvert, since he would put me at ease with his humbleness and self-deprecating humor. I trust David more than I trust Bentley. David is likelier to ask curious questions, keenly listen, and care.

While we're here: A common myth needs to be dispelled about introverts and extroverts related to what type of personality excels at networking events. Public opinion falsely assumes that introverts are poor networkers, while extroverts are brilliant networkers. It's not necessarily true. This grossly unfair broad brushstroke often sets up both introverts and extroverts for failure by creating false personal narratives.

If an introvert is doubtful about their ability to engage skillfully at networking events, chances are ripe for a self-fulfilling prophecy to take hold, and they're going to exude a lack of confidence that will cause their fears to come true.

Introverts are often trusted because of their genuine interest in others and their talent of staying present in the moment. If you are an introvert, rest assured that you can shine brightly at networking events.

Extroverts, meanwhile, may have an outsized belief in their abilities, as was true of Bentley. Blindly and blithely, Bentley alienated people, which is the antithesis of the networking goal.

Overcome Networking Blunder #5:
Poor Business Card Exchanges

Be mindful of the way you present, receive, and stow business cards. When you put the following into practice, you set yourself apart with high distinction:

- **Presenting Your Card.** Present your card only after the beginning of a relationship or after meaningful conversation has occurred. It's premature to hand someone a card before trust is established. Instead of presenting the card out of the gate, wait. It's nice to do this at the end of an initial meeting since it will be better received and allows for a smoother closure. Either a one-handed or two-handed presentation of your card is acceptable. However, it's become universally preferred to use the more formal way of strongly presenting with two hands. You simply get noticed—and in a more favorable light. If you choose to present or receive with only one hand, always use the right hand, never the left hand. (In some cultures, the left hand is considered dirty.) If you're at an office, always present your card to the receptionist to show respect and to also ensure that your contact information is correctly shared with whomever you're meeting. Present with the text about the person (not the company) facing the recipient and don't hand it out like you're dealing cards in a poker game. Finally, avoid over-packing your cards with too much pomp and fluff and try to use standard-sized cards, as they are easier to stow. Keep in mind that if you're at a business meal or gala, you should exchange cards before or after the meal since it's not in good form to do so during the meal.

- **Receiving a Card.** Again, two hands are preferred. Create a moment. Take time to thoughtfully read the card, show interest, and perhaps ask a curious question or offer a genuine compliment about its contents. It will please the presenter that you cared enough to absorb the card. A business card represents a person's dreams, passions, goals, and worries, and it should be treated with the utmost respect. Consequently, it's in poor form to impolitely write on a business card in the presence of your counterpart—this can be perceived as defacing their card. If you need to add a cell number or something else to the card, make a note in your phone, then transfer the information to the card when you're not in the presence of your counterpart.

- **Stowing a Card.** It demonstrates respect when you stow the card in a proper card case or portfolio. If you're not carrying either, wait until your counterpart walks away before you shove it in your back pocket. If you stow the card in front of your counterpart in a place of respect, their perception of you will be a respectful one. Also, never insert your card in a thank-you note to avoid the perception of being disingenuous.

Touchless Business Card Exchange in Today's Digital World

If you're caught out and about without your business cards, you can always use the LinkedIn app on your smartphone. Connect with the LinkedIn QR code by tapping the search bar, which reveals four icons to the right of the search bar. These four dots are the gateway to electronically exchanging your LinkedIn profile and contact information with your counterpart. Once the code page is accessed, you have the capability of mutually scanning and sharing your QR codes by clicking phones, assuming they also have a LinkedIn app, which most people do. Your counterpart can then scan your QR code, which prominently appears on the LinkedIn Code page. A Share My Code feature is also available.

Pre-Event, At the Event, and Post-Event Strategies

ENGAGE

Once upon a time,
unfortunate blunders were made . . .

Carefully review the examples from Week 1 ENGAGE to refresh your memory of the common blunders that occur at networking events:

1. The Dread of Networking Events

2. Waiting to Network Until You Need to

3. Beware of the 3 Bs: Bar, Buffet, and Buddies

4. The Myth—Introverts Are Lousy Networkers

5. Poor Business Card Exchanges

ENLIGHTEN

with Ms. Tiffany's Epiphanies®

Have you ever regretted not taking full advantage of a networking event? You're not alone. Like public speaking, networking is often equal parts necessary and dreaded. Many dread these performances because introducing yourself to strangers and spending time chitchatting is exhausting after a long workday.

However, they are necessary and invaluable opportunities for growing your career and/or business via building relationship capital.

To help achieve success and enjoy these events more than you do now, change your mindset. Instead of thinking that your success depends solely on your behaviors during the networking event, think in terms of three phases: *Pre, During,* and *Post.*

PRE-EVENT NETWORKING STRATEGIES

1. Secure the guest list.

Request an attendee roster from the event organizer in advance of the event. Identify the high-value attendees, prioritize them, and then do your research. You can even simply take a picture of the attendees' nametags at the registration table before the event and then do a quick LinkedIn peek of their profile. That's better than walking in cold. Information is power.

2. Do your research and create a plan.

On LinkedIn, ascertain the backgrounds, group affiliations, hobbies, thought leaders followed, and media posts of targeted attendees. Discover shared interests and commonalities that would spark meaningful conversation and connection.

3. Invite a wing person.

Having a partner to motivate you to follow through with your commitment to attend the event and mitigate awkwardness can be a lifesaver. Share your goals about with whom you need to engage. Return the favor to your wing person. Soon you'll have qualified new people to add to your expanding networking circle.

4. Embrace a positive self-narrative.

Prior to the event, have a sunny disposition and an optimistic mindset when thinking or talking about attending the event. After all, your outlook determines your outcome. Would it have been more convenient to attend the networking event during your workday? Probably so. However, other business gets conducted then so at least you're on the invite list.

AT THE EVENT NETWORKING STRATEGIES

1. Arrive early.

It sounds counterintuitive, but being among the first attendees rewards you with the advantage of easily engaging with conversation partners before they've settled into an established clique.

2. Move with purpose—and notify your face.

When you enter the room, you're noticed more than you think. Attendees will naturally glance toward the door several times over the course of an event. A few seconds before you enter, notify your face that you are pleased to be there by putting on a soft smile, thereby making you more approachable. After you enter, step to the side to allow yourself time to assess the layout of the room and the people to meet. When you decide where to start working the room, move with purpose. Wandering aimlessly, using your phone as a crutch, gives the impression of insecurity. Incidentally, indulging too soon in the 3 Bs (bar, buffet, and buddies) is the kiss of death. It communicates unprofessionalism and a lack of care.

3. Join groups smoothly.

As you approach groups, always keep your right hand free so you can readily shake hands. Search for the groups with open body language and friendly demeanors. Never interrupt two people who are seriously engaged with sustained eye contact. Find one friendly gatekeeper in a group, a person who will make eye contact with you and welcome you into the group conversation. Smile at your designated gatekeeper as you move toward them and say four magical words: "May I join you?"

Introduce yourself and share your employer's name. Shake hands with each person, squarely facing each one, belly button to belly button. Pivot from one person to another as you say their name. "Steve, it's a pleasure." Hearing one's own name releases a feel-good chemical in the brain every time. If your gatekeeper is unaware of their responsibility to divulge the topic of conversation with you, take the initiative to say, "I hope I'm not interrupting. Please continue. What are we discussing?" Do your part and keenly listen.

A Personal Share: I can't underscore enough the importance of not interrupting two people seriously engaged in conversation. Recently, I was engaged with sustained eye contact and serious discussion with one person at a networking event. This friend was sharing how her brother was terminally ill, and I was sharing about my mom's recent graduation to Heaven. Another person innocently and jovially interrupted us to say hello. Words cannot express how off-putting and awkward the interruption was . . . for all three of us. Be courteous by noticing engaged body language. Seek open groups to join.

4. Embark on a *Help Hunt.*

Have a goal of giving without expecting anything in return. Be a helpful resource and a solution to the dilemmas that others might have. Play a mind game with yourself in which you're on a mission, a *Help Hunt,* to seek at least one way to help each conversation partner you meet. Albert Einstein stated, "Try not to become a person of success, but rather try to become a person of value." How can you add value to their life *after* this networking event? This will make you "sticky" (memorable) in your new acquaintance's eyes. A few examples include:

- Find them or a loved one employment if they are in transition.

- Refer business to them or invite them to be your guest at a future networking event.

- Write a LinkedIn recommendation about their work.

5. Be *large and in charge* with body language.

Experts suggest that far greater weight is placed on body language during a new encounter than either on content or voice tone. For example, change your stance so that your feet are spread apart a bit wider than your shoulders, putting your weight mostly in your heels and not your toes.

6. Wear your name badge properly.

Your name badge should be high and right, not low and right, and not high and left. This placement around the upper lapel/shoulder area allows you both to shake hands using a seamless eye movement along the line of sight traveling from your clasped hands, up the arm, catching the name, and smoothly settling into sustained eye contact. This allows both parties to avoid awkward breaks in eye contact to search for the name. Furthermore, a good rule of thumb when someone asks you to join in on a photo opportunity at an event is to set aside your name badge and beverage for a cleaner look.

7. Leave groups smoothly.

Too much consternation is placed on excusing oneself from the company of others. Simply say, "I need to excuse myself, but it's been a pleasure meeting everyone. Enjoy the evening." Shake hands with everyone and remember to mention each name as you are shaking hands and bidding farewell. There is no sweeter sound to a person's ears than their own name.

8. Politely escape when someone is monopolizing you.

Have you ever been accosted at a networking event and held hostage? When a person is monopolizing you in conversation, it feels like you are being held captive for hours instead of minutes. How do you escape politely without being offensive? Once again, it's all in the body language. First, extend your hand for a handshake and with a smiling face say, "I enjoyed meeting you. Let's stay in touch and connect on LinkedIn." The mere physical gesture of initiating a handshake puts it out into the universe politely, yet emphatically, that the exchange is over. Second, consider inviting another person into your conversation. Make a proper introduction to the newcomer by providing an engaging conversation starter. This gives you a springboard to exit since they will now be immersed in a new engagement.

A Word to the Wise: Be wary of the tired excuses people overuse to exit a conversation. People can see through ploys to jump ship, so don't leave the lasting impression that you are disingenuous. Avoid these platitudes:

- "I'm starved. Want to check out the food?"
- "Let's get you another drink."
- "Do you know where the restrooms are?"

A MESSAGE TO MY SISTERS

Women tend to undermine their credibility by condensing their physical stature—hunching, crossing knee over knee, pinning elbows in close to sides. Avoid self-calming, nervous gestures like the plague (adjusting or twirling hair or jewelry, playing with your collar, and placing your hands in the fig-leaf position, which is clasping hands in front or in your pockets). Widen your stance, push back your shoulders, avoid a subservient head tilt, lift your chin, and make a statement of relaxed confidence.

POST-EVENT NETWORKING STRATEGIES

1. Use technology to streamline your networking efforts.

In your phone, immediately make notes of *"memorables"* from each interaction at the event. Better yet, download a trusted app that allows you access to an efficient, organized system for your networking efforts. Religiously utilize it at every turn. This pivot toward using an app to organize your networking efforts will be transformational in building a stellar reputation and will prevent you from missing opportunities and overlooking touchpoints. Do research on the plethora of networking apps available and select one that best suits your style and needs. These apps make it easy for you to:

- Organize your connections for easier communication, via text or email

- Establish goals for frequency of contacting each connection and get reminders of when to do so

- View timelines of past touchpoints

- Receive reminder notifications about your network's milestones like birthdays, anniversaries, graduations, and weddings

- Avoid embarrassment by helping you remember details about leads, prospects, clients, and centers of influence

- Get updates on your connections' social media postings for thoughtful follow-up

You may think you'll remember these details and reach out to your contacts on time, but you won't without a system. People are wowed when details of their lives are remembered because it makes them feel valued.

2. Reach out within forty-eight hours.

At the minimum, promptly touch base with your new acquaintance by email or a personalized LinkedIn invite. If you really wish to set yourself apart with distinction, pick up the phone and invite them to coffee.

3. Promises made, promises kept.

During your Help Hunt, you no doubt made a promise to do something to help a new acquaintance add value to their life or to the life of someone near and dear to them. Keep your word. All you have in business is your reputation, which is the glue to building trust. When you build trust, you build relationships. When you build meaningful relationships, you build a solid network. At the end of the day, meaningful relationship-building is what you depend on for success. Whether you promise to help someone find employment or email them about the brand of your shoes, honor your word and follow through. It's amazing how fast word travels when you don't, and that impacts your reputation.

The Forgotten Network— Dormant Relationships

ENGAGE

Once upon a time,
unfortunate blunders were made . . .

A PERSONAL SHARE: MY LINKEDIN EXCHANGE WITH A COLLEGE FRIEND

LinkedIn kept prompting me to connect with various people in its "People You May Know" window that appears whenever I log into my account.

On this particular day, LinkedIn suggested the profile that belonged to Matt, a dormant friendship from my college days at Miami University. I hadn't thought about Matt in years, but Matt was a good guy, so why not? I sent a LinkedIn invite to connect with him. He was now an executive for a major cleaning company. Perhaps there might be some synergies between our two organizations, and it would be fun to say hi after all these years.

Hi Matt,

You may recall that we were friends at Miami University. We have a mutual buddy in Mike Alby, who remains one of my best friends. I was wondering if you would like to connect on LI in the spirit of remembering the good old days when life was simple? Ha.

Best,
Tiffany

Hi Tiffany,

Of course, I remember you and gladly accept your invite to connect. How are you? What are you up to these days?

Matt

Hi Matt,

Life is good. I now own my own business called the Cincinnati Etiquette & Leadership Institute, LLC (CELI), after working years in the banking industry. I kept getting pulled by a calling to found a company that offers business etiquette and professional development training. This training empowers clients, nationally and internationally, to employ the strategies of modern business etiquette that sets clients apart with excellence and high distinction. I like to think of CELI as a way to breathe new life into a lost art. Happily, my vision was enthusiastically embraced as a fresh competitive advantage in the workplace. How is your family doing?

Best,
Tiffany

Long Story Short

For a few months, I took special notice on LinkedIn when Matt would post about the importance of helping special needs children. I started sending him relevant research articles on this topic. I also would like, comment, or share his posts about the worthy causes he was advocating for to help him spread the word and gain awareness. Matt appreciated my others-focused approach. He also appreciated my genuine interest to help him spread the word since this was a mission near and dear to his family's heart.

After a bit, I reached out again.

Tiffany:

> Hi Matt,
>
> You have done quite well for yourself, and I would love to learn more about what you do and how your journey has transpired. I have a strong passion for the mission of my company and always appreciate an opportunity to share how we help empower others to be their finest selves. Perhaps there would be some synergies that we could explore between our two organizations. Would you like to meet in person sometime?

Matt:

> Agreed. Let's get together!

Matt and I met in his office, and the conversation flowed easily and effortlessly, as though no time had passed. We had fun reminiscing about our days at our beloved alma mater. The good news is that Matt did indeed engage my company's training services—supporting his organization's vendor diversity goals since I owned a woman-owned WBE-certified business.

Do you have any dormant relationships that perhaps you would like to reactivate? LinkedIn is a professional gold mine to start searching for those forgotten ties.

ENLIGHTEN

with Ms. Tiffany's Epiphanies®

WHY MAKE NETWORKING DIFFICULT?

Have you ever known someone who insists on taking the windiest, most difficult road when an easier, straighter path is staring them in the face? Or a person who refuses to stop and ask for directions when they're completely lost? Let's take some of the *work* out of *networking* for you.

Modern Networking: Rekindle the Forgotten Network

Conventional networking requires persuading acquaintances to literally buy into you and your business. But first you must cultivate these acquaintances through building trust and likeability.

With the profound changes wrought by the pandemic and ever-evolving technology, is there still a place for this traditional form of networking?

Absolutely . . . mostly.

Yes, the old-school skills of building relationships still apply, but they should also incorporate some modern strategies. One of these is nurturing your *forgotten network*, which can give you a competitive edge with less work. In other words, never burn a bridge, because there may come a day when you want to reengage these former ties.

David Burkus, an expert on leadership and innovation and author of *Friend of a Friend*, brilliantly captures this concept:

> Much of the conventional networking advice is focused on reaching out and meeting brand-new people. While that is a noble goal . . . and new connections are likely to provide novel and valuable opportunities, research encourages us to consider old, dormant ties in our network before spending so much energy investing in new relationships. . . . Reactivating old connections is much faster than building a brand-new relationship from scratch.

Why build new when you may already have key existing connections buried in your past? Let's generate additional value from these relationships. We'll learn how in Week 4.

Download a Networking App

ELEVATE

Learn by Doing Exercise

FIND THE NETWORKING APP THAT'S RIGHT FOR YOU

Leverage technology by going online to investigate the world of networking apps. Download the app that's right for you but use it with consistency. Then enjoy the *oohs* and *aahs* that come from making others feel special because you remembered a key detail about them—all while positioning yourself to look like a consummate professional.

Jot down your goals for the app and any pain points you have encountered in networking that the app can help alleviate. Keep these in mind as you sleuth for just the right app for you.

Executive Presence and Authentic Leadership

What Executive Presence Is Not

ENGAGE

Once upon a time,
unfortunate blunders were made . . .

I would like to introduce to you seven leaders who lack executive presence. Do any of the following profiles remind you of yourself?

Each of the leaders you're about to meet is glaringly missing one of the *7 Characteristics of Executive Presence* (EP) needed to be a successful leader. Each of these characteristics will be explained in the next ENLIGHTEN section, but for now, let's examine what executive presence is not. The end game for a polished and persuasive leader with professional swagger is to ultimately possess all seven characteristics, so let's dissect one characteristic at a time.

Note: You'll have your chance to fill in the blanks below in Week 4 after you learn about the 7 Cs of EP in the next section. However, the seven questions about the leaders are being posed here without the requirement of filling in the blanks so that you begin pondering each leader's missing EP characteristic.

1. **Larry the leader** wasn't exactly cool in a crisis as he tried to address his talent's low morale. And hiring his unemployed

brother-in-law to impress his new bride despite the company's anti-nepotism policy didn't exactly help. Instead, the rumor mill started to churn with rampant gossip about Larry's violation of the nepotism policy. Larry panicked. He took to the keyboard to write a scathing email to all employees justifying why his wife's brother was a good hire.

Which one of the 7 Cs of Executive Presence is Larry lacking ?

2. **Lynn the leader** had her own agenda in managing the team. After the COVID-19 vaccine had been distributed and employees were returning to the office, Lynn would zone out in her one-on-one meetings when employees shared the highlights and lowlights of their time in quarantine. Lynn never followed up to ask a curious question or offer to assist. She sat through these discussions with the secret hope that they could all return to normal business routines without her having to hear her team's personal woes.

Which one of the 7 Cs of Executive Presence is Lynn lacking ?

3. **Louise the leader** welcomed her team back after working remotely for nearly a year. While her cohorts in the Chamber's CEO Roundtable tried to adapt and stay current by learning about new agile leadership models, growth mindsets during crisis, and safety protocols for in-person work

environments, Louise refused such nimbleness. When she attended internal employee gatherings, she rarely asked questions of her workforce. She didn't remember their names, let alone the names of their families. She was overwhelmed by the new landscape after the pandemic and didn't seem to be concerned for the welfare of her workforce.

Which one of the 7Cs of Executive Presence is Louise lacking ❓

---

4. **Leonard the leader** often used lame attempts at self-deprecating humor, comparing his attention span to a squirrel or a goldfish because of his lack of focus. He wore a smartwatch, which constantly competed for his attention with pings, email notifications, text arrivals, and Twitter feeds. Never immersed in a conversation, he was always distracted by the next ping or someone new walking into the room.

Which one of the 7Cs of Executive Presence is Leonard lacking ❓

---

5. **Lucy the leader** would present herself in the smallest manner possible, taking up as little space as she could. Shrinking in stature, she would speak with her hands clasped in front of her, pulling her elbows close to her sides, hunching her shoulders, and keeping her head down to avoid sustained eye contact. When faced with a tough decision, she'd defer

to her direct reports instead of making a tough call that might ruffle feathers.

Which one of the 7Cs of Executive Presence is Lucy lacking ❓

6. **Lydia the leader** always explained in nauseating detail how to design a clock even if she was only asked the time. Lydia was consumed with providing excessive amounts of context and background before getting to the point. Her messaging was longwinded and convoluted. Often, by the time she finished speaking, her counterpart had forgotten the purpose of the original conversation.

Which one of the 7Cs of Executive Presence is Lydia lacking ❓

7. **Logan the leader** always promised the moon but never delivered. Whether or not his intentions were sincere, nobody could tell. All anyone knew is that when Logan promised to submit a report in a week, return a call immediately, or have his team deliver something, it never happened on time or failed to occur at all. Either the dog ate his homework or there was silence following an unfulfilled promise.

Which one of the 7Cs of Executive Presence is Logan lacking ❓

Executive Presence
and Why Leaders Need It

Heads up, leaders! If you commit one of these blunders, then your legitimacy as a leader may be compromised, and this affects your upward mobility.

A smart way to go from *good* to *great* leadership is by cultivating authenticity. Start by understanding what it means to not be authentic. Avoid these pitfalls of inauthenticity:

- Not fulfilling your commitments or delivering on your promises

- Insincerity in nurturing relationships

- Not valuing the opinions of others

- Saying things that you don't mean or telling half-truths just to puff others up, manipulate their thoughts or actions, or take pressure off yourself

- Being closed-minded, thus limiting your access to new ideas and innovation

- Yearning for the glory—creating agendas that only benefit you

- Being a people-pleaser to avoid offering honest candor

- Compromising your values and integrity for advancement or popularity

- Withholding resources or wisdom for fear of being outshined

- Treating others differently based on what they can do for you

- Depending too heavily on affirmation from others rather than confidently believing in your own strengths

- Being thin-skinned and taking things too personally

- Being distracted and only partially listening

- Upholding one set of standards for you, and another set of standards for others

- Acting differently in private than you do in public

- Hoarding credit and not giving credit where it is due

- Not empathizing with or validating another's concerns

ENLIGHTEN

with Ms. Tiffany's Epiphanies®

Visualize a person who drips class, likeability, and refinement from every pore of their body, like no one else on their finest day.

Picture someone you hold in the highest regard who effortlessly projects a commanding presence. It's difficult to define executive presence, but when it walks into the room, heads turn and eyes shift. Suddenly, this person becomes the center of attention—the one everyone wants to get to know. What is their secret? Were they born with this alluring swagger, or did they acquire it somehow? This person represents your new exemplary role model to whom you aspire to reach your higher self.

"Humble leaders recognize that they are not on earth to see how important they can become but to see how much difference they can make in the lives of others."

—LEADERSHIP FIRST

WHAT IS EXECUTIVE PRESENCE (EP)?

- The ability to engage, inspire, influence, align, and motivate people to act with high standards of character and style

- The internal convergence of focused speech, body language, and movements that are exquisitely synchronized to make you compelling and commanding

- Your professional swagger

WHY DOES A LEADER NEED EXECUTIVE PRESENCE AND CAN IT BE LEARNED?

Simply put, executive presence makes you a stronger leader . . . one who commands more respect and motivates employees to reach shared goals. A leader with powerful executive presence builds trust more easily, earns more credibility, and influences team members to achieve business results.

By conducting a self-inventory on a consistent basis with a heightened self-awareness of the following seven characteristics of executive presence, you can cultivate a growth mindset.

THE 7 CS OF EXECUTIVE PRESENCE

1. Composure/Calmness

Are you someone who is cool in a crisis and calm during an emotional situation? Are you self-aware and self-restrained? Then you have **composure and calmness.**

2. Connectivity

Do you feel compassion and empathy for others and resist the temptation to focus on your needs or mistreatment? Do you engage others easily and make them feel comfortable so their higher selves emerge? Then you have **connectivity.**

3. Curiosity

Are you an others-focused person, asking probing questions that amplify and energize others? Do you consider yourself a lifelong learner and set out to intentionally learn something new? Then you have **curiosity.**

4. Charisma

Do you have an energy that draws others to you? Are you a keen listener who stays present in the moment and is not easily distracted? Then you have **charisma.**

5. Confidence

Are you large and in charge with how you present yourself nonverbally? Are you decisive about making tough decisions and rarely look back to reconsider the choice? Then you have **confidence.**

6. Credibility

Are you authentic, sincere, transparent, and genuine? Do you keep your word? Then you have **credibility.**

7. Conciseness

Do you say things crisply and succinctly? Are you brief, brilliant, and gone when you speak or write? Are you clear with your messaging and not verbose? Then you have **conciseness.**

Executive presence can be learned if you aren't born with it, but it takes a heightened self-awareness and self-restraint coupled with persistent practice. As you inventory how you fare with each of these 7 Cs, you may find yourself to be more adept with some and less skilled with others. This self-analysis should evolve into an ongoing reevaluation that will consistently elevate you to the next level. Routinely identifying your strengths and areas of improvement, followed by rebalancing them to mitigate your limitations, will accelerate progress. Even small tweaks to your areas of improvement will catapult your quest toward achieving executive presence. Periodically asking trusted advisors for honest feedback of how you rank with the 7 Cs is invaluable to keeping you in check. The higher you advance up the corporate ladder, the less feedback for improvement you'll receive, since people get intimidated by authority. This can stunt your growth, so be aware. Therefore, recruiting trusted advisors who will be forthright with you regarding your executive presence is worth its weight in gold for positioning yourself for upward mobility.

Ignite a Growth Mindset with 2 Power Traits

When authenticity and self-compassion are not engaged through-out a leader's journey, a leader risks becoming their own worst enemy, as seen in this graphic:

2 POWER TRAITS EMBRACED BY TODAY'S SMART LEADERS

1. Authenticity

Authenticity is the quality of being worthy of acceptance, not false or copied. It's the state of coming from the heart; of being trustworthy, transparent, genuine, or reliable. Authenticity is being true to one's personality, spirit, or character.

Leaders, Slippery Slope Ahead—Watch Your Blind Spots!

Executive Presence won't do you or your career any good if you aren't authentic at every turn in your behavior, thought, words, and heart. It's not enough to robotically go through the motions of executing the 7 Cs of EP, unless authenticity and self-compassion are interwoven throughout your 7 Cs. If you aren't genuine, then your legitimacy as a leader will be compromised, which undermines your credibility. Furthermore, you will be hard pressed to withstand the pressures and critical judgments inevitably cast in every leader's journey. Authenticity grants leaders a free hall pass and an extra dose of patience from others when leaders need grace the most. People are more apt to forgive an authentic leader trying their best when the leader inevitably fails by making a judgment error, committing a communication blunder, or underestimating a well-intentioned employee.

What's the Fallout of Inauthentic Leadership?

Candidly, your team will smell a rat. You will breed distrust and suspicion, coupled with resistance to following your lead. You won't be taken as seriously, and it may feel like each day you are climbing a mountain with bricks strapped to your shoes. Simply put, being inauthentic serves as your looming roadblock to success. If you are leading with authenticity, empower your team with it. Frequently ask your team members, "How can I help you reach that goal? What resources or flexibility can I arrange for you to better accomplish that project with all that you have on your plate?" Avoid asking, "Why hasn't your goal been reached?" Once you take the time to ask thought-provoking questions of others, observe the pressure valve of relief and uplifted spirit in your employees' faces. This mere pivot in your narrative demonstrates genuine concern and a willingness to serve as their catalyst for success. This approach will foster an environment of trust and loyalty that will make you unstoppable as a leader whose goal is to motivate everyone to row in the same direction.

> " If you are leading with authenticity, empower your team with it.

2. Self-Compassion

Self-compassion is defined as judging yourself after a setback or failure in a gentle manner that protects self-worth, promotes recovery, and invites discovery.

Further—and this is important—*failure does not have to be fatal.*

The critical trust that leaders earn over time from team members can be instantly severed by underestimating the power of self-compassion. Why? Because you miss opportunities to learn something new and contribute greater value. Self-compassion is an essential yet often overlooked leadership trait. Hands down, there is no finer teacher in life than the mistakes we make. How we treat ourselves afterward affects the lessons we learn and the wisdom we acquire. A common myth that needs dispelling is that self-compassion equates to fluff and frivolity. When you give yourself a break after making a mistake, it can be misconstrued as letting yourself off the hook, throwing yourself a pity party, protecting your bruised ego, or deflecting the wrong onto others. This thinking is flawed. Self-compassion encourages one's mindset to remain open, paving the way to learn invaluable lessons that could not be learned had the failure not occurred. If you aren't failing occasionally as a leader (or as a human, for that matter), you're either suffering from delusional perfectionism or playing it too safe by not incurring any risks to make a difference. Either way, live and learn . . . and grow. Avoid the trap that awaits you when you're too hard on yourself.

Think about how uplifting it is when a friend consoles and encourages you as you show vulnerability by seeking their support after failing. If we would treat ourselves in the same gracious manner as our friends treat us when we're down, we would reap the benefits that self-compassion sows in our leadership journey a lot sooner.

Why Is Self-Compassion Important to a Leader's Growth Mindset?

Leaders are human, and humans make mistakes. We're all perpetual works in progress until the day we leave this world. Failure can be a catalyst for success, and forgiveness can be a gateway to peace. The most productive and well-adjusted leaders are the ones who acknowledge their mistakes yet make the choice to let them go. They forgive not only themselves, but more importantly, they have the decency

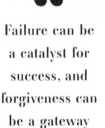

> Failure can be a catalyst for success, and forgiveness can be a gateway to peace.

to forgive others when wronged. They realize that this self-grace when one forgives oneself for making a blunder will preempt risky, aggressive behavior that has the potential of manifesting itself into precarious actions. How we cope with these setbacks determines our outcome. Do leaders shut down? No. Do leaders hold grudges? No. Do leaders give second, third, and fourth chances? Absolutely.

After committing a blunder, do you use this as a time of self-reflection and discovery to make yourself better? Or do you beat yourself up until you're black-and-blue and eventually succumb to defeatism? The first option is the stronger choice for building resilience and resolve.

Studies show that self-compassion enhances professional development because it promotes higher self-esteem and a growth mindset. Instead of self-flagellation consuming a person when a setback occurs, the person who engages in self-compassion is empowered to give themselves the gift of a second chance to excel. The leader welcomes the misstep as an opportunity to become a more genuine leader who is relatable to others when they fail.

Carol Dweck is a brilliant American psychologist and pioneering researcher. In an article by *Mindset Works*—a company based on the research of Dweck and co-founder Lisa Blackwell—we learn about the importance of two types of mindsets that can make or break a successful leader:

> Dr. Dweck coined the terms fixed mindset and growth mindset to describe the underlying beliefs people have about learning and intelligence. When students believe they can get smarter, they understand that effort makes

them stronger. Therefore, they put in extra time and effort, and that leads to higher achievement.[8]

What Makes Leaders Believe They CAN Get Smarter?

A leader with a growth or abundance mindset believes that good can come from the bad in mistakes made. They believe in what Dr. Dweck calls "the power of yet." The power of yet looks at a setback from an optimistic lens—not as an irreversible disaster, but as a situation that isn't quite rife for development. This allows you the opportunity to pivot and try something else that may indeed work.

Leaders who possess growth mindsets:

- Embrace new challenges

- Appreciate constructive feedback

- View failures as learning opportunities

- Emphasize efforts, not just outcomes

- Embody a positive attitude

They believe that effort is part of the leader's journey to reach self-fulfillment. Praising effort over outcome generates positive results.

What Makes Leaders Believe They CAN'T Get Smarter?

Some leaders limit themselves with a fixed mindset. Leaders with fixed mindsets:

---

[8] "Dr. Dweck's Research into Growth Mindset Changed Education Forever," www.mindsetworks.com /science, accessed February 22, 2022.

- Give up early and easily

- Stick only to what they know because *it's always been done this way, and they cannot change*

- Feel hopeless and overwhelmed with challenges

- Avoid challenges, conflict with others, and creative problem solving

- Reject feedback and constructive criticism

- Need constant reassurance

- Blame a setback on other people or circumstances because conflict or unfortunate occurrences are never their fault

Communications specialist Andrew Fletcher Cole captures the merits of a growth mindset exceptionally well:

> Adopting a growth mindset is, for me, an antidote to letting "failure" rule my life. Moreover, it allows me to turn setbacks and disappointments into learning, looking beyond my perceived deficiencies to enter a world of possibility.[9]

What Do Self-Compassion and a Growth Mindset Have to Do with Each Other?

Everything! Self-compassion opens the door for self-improvement because self-doubt is snuffed out. When self-doubt is stifled, fertile ground allows the seeds of a growth mindset to take hold. As a result, a good leader transforms into a great leader.

---

[9] Andrew Fletcher Cole, "Adopting a Growth Mindset," www.linkedin.com/pulse/adopting-growth -mindset-andrew-fletcher-cole, accessed February 22, 2022.

Self-compassion allows a leader to embrace learning from constructive criticism and candid feedback. Leaders are, thereafter, better equipped to climb a steeper learning curve and contribute more value.

A Big Bonus to Your Leadership Skill Set

Self-compassion often jump-starts possessing compassion for others. You gain good practice in learning how to treat others well when you treat yourself well. It's like airplane safety protocol, where parents are advised to put on their own oxygen masks before helping their children. Tone at the top matters. When a leader serves as a strong role model in exemplifying self-compassion and compassion for others, their authenticity teaches the gold standard of great leadership.

> You gain good practice in learning how to treat others well when you treat yourself well.

Lesson Learned?

Give yourself a break when you make a mistake and view mistakes as life's bridges to enlightenment. You will earn greater trust and receive credit for inspiring a culture of innovation and lifelong learning that ultimately leads to higher levels of productivity and bottom-line results.

Avoid the Pitfalls of Inauthentic Leadership

ELEVATE

Learn by Doing Exercises

1. ACT AUTHENTICALLY

Heighten your self-awareness and self-restraint. Be vigilant about being authentic. Fill in the blanks by providing five of your own examples of inauthenticity that you've either personally observed in other leaders or committed yourself (if you need inspiration, review the list of pitfalls in Week 2):

_____

_____

_____

_____

_____

2. PRACTICE SELF-COMPASSION AND REWRITE YOUR STORY

Journal about a time where you unfairly flogged yourself in the past and didn't exercise self-compassion. Describe the mistake, the way you treated yourself, and the impact the mistake and your treatment of yourself manifested in an unfavorable way. Ask yourself, "Were there any long-term consequences, personally or professionally, that resulted in lower amounts of executive presence or negative outcomes?"

Next, rewrite the experience, applying the aforementioned principles of self-compassion. What would have been a healthier way to recover from your mistake, bounce back more quickly, and exude more executive presence? Keep a thick rubber band on your desk or on your wrist with the word *self-compassion* boldly written on it. It will serve as a daily reminder to give yourself a break to bounce back with resilience.

3. ASSESS YOURSELF AND DETERMINE YOUR EXECUTIVE PRESENCE

In Week 2, you were given the 7 Cs of Executive Presence. Every three months, evaluate yourself on your evolving areas of improvement and strengths by completing the following:

This quarter, my top two areas for improvement regarding the 7 Cs are:

_____ and

_____

This quarter, my top two strengths to celebrate regarding the 7 C s are:

_____ and

_____

This quarter, I will let go of the following three failures by learning from them and being self-compassionate:

Failure #1 _____

_____

Lesson Learned from Failure #1 _____

_____

Failure #2 _____

_____

Lesson Learned from Failure #2 _____

_____

Failure #3 _____

_____

Lesson Learned from Failure #3 _____

_____

4. TEST YOUR UNDERSTANDING OF WHAT THE SEVEN LEADERS LACK IN EP AND WHY

Which of the 7 Cs do the seven leaders lack?

The 7 Cs of Executive Presence (EP) include:

1. Composure/Calmness

2. Connectivity

3. Curiosity

4. Charisma

5. Confidence

6. Credibility

7. Conciseness

First, refresh your memory by rereading the definitions of each of the 7 Cs of EP in Week 2. Second, reacquaint yourself with each leader's blunder described in Week 1. Third, fill in the blanks and test your understanding of Executive Presence. The Answer Key is upside down at the end of this section. Which one of the 7 Cs of Executive Presence are the leaders lacking?

Note: Pay attention—the leaders' names have purposely been mixed up.

Larry lacks _____

Leonard lacks _____

Logan lacks _____

Louise lacks _____

Lucy lacks _____

Lydia lacks _____

Lynn lacks _____

Answer Key:

- Larry lacks composure/calmness.
- Leonard lacks charisma.
- Logan lacks credibility.
- Louise lacks curiosity.
- Lucy lacks confidence.
- Lydia lacks conciseness.
- Lynn lacks connectivity. (Curiosity could also apply.)

Virtual Communication and the Inclusive Remote Workplace

New Greeting Etiquette Emerges in a Touchless Society

ENGAGE

Once upon a time,
unfortunate blunders were made . . .

At its core, modern business etiquette is all about seamlessly engaging in sophisticated behavior using high-caliber communication skills to preserve decorum, create favorable impressions, set yourself apart with excellence, put others at ease, and, most importantly, allow meaningful relationship-building to take root. However, COVID-19 has altered how we interact and added entire new platforms for engagement. Along with these changes, new opportunities to commit mistakes that weaken relationship-building and impact your bottom line are evolving.

As of this writing, it's hard to say when we will fully return to a sense of normality and what changes wrought by COVID-19 and its variants will remain. Nonetheless, we must adapt to the next norm and be nimbly prepared for at least some of these changes to take hold in the foreseeable future.

> **Even the simple act of asking shows courtesy.**

To start, let's focus on favorable first impressions. As the world reexamines social customs in light of our new understanding of viral epidemics, how do we engage in touchless greetings while still enjoying the merits of a physical connection?

Importantly, we must show respect and empathy for the diverse range of preferences people have about greetings. Each acquaintance will have a personal preference as to how they wish to be greeted. To touch or not to touch—that is the question. Address the elephant in the room by inquiring about their preference up front. After all, we can't read minds to determine where others stand on their greeting preferences. Even the simple act of asking shows courtesy. No matter their preference, you can put your body language to work to establish genuine connection—even a touchless greeting can still convey warmth.

That being said, the following blunders should be avoided.

Greeting Blunder #1: The Fist Bump

Fist bumps are thought to be more hygienic than handshakes due to the shorter duration of contact and smaller contact area. While baseball players are famously big fans of the fist bump and forearm press, it's best to leave the fist bump at the ballpark—it doesn't convey the formality and professionalism appropriate for a business setting.

Greeting Blunder #2: The Elbow Bump

The concerns associated with the fist bump apply to the elbow bump as well, plus one more: awkwardness. Why? First, it's difficult to telegraph this specific gesture to another person, resulting in discomfort when they leave you hanging, unsure of their intentions and how you should respond. Second, when two people engage, their bodies should be squared up, meaning your shoulders need to square with their shoulders, and your belly button should be aligned with theirs. This body language conveys keen attention and full engagement. To initiate an elbow bump, one must naturally turn to the side, giving the impression of disengaging from the conversation. These elements make for a clumsy encounter not destined to create a favorable impression.

ENLIGHTEN

with Ms. Tiffany's Epiphanies®

NEW GREETING ETIQUETTE EMERGES

As noted above, different people will have different sensitivities when it comes to physical contact, and we must respect their choices as part of our others-focused approach. And yet, as much as we want to stay healthy, we also do not want to sacrifice human connection. To set yourself apart with rare professional courtesy, follow this new greeting etiquette by saying, "I want to be respectful of your preference with greetings. Are you comfortable with shaking hands or are you not there yet?" If they reply in the negative, politely affirm their choice.

If a touchless greeting is preferred, fully engage with other nonverbal cues. Smile, make sustained eye contact, raise your eyebrows, and place a hand over your heart as you say, "I wish we could shake hands (or hug). Hopefully, someday soon." The hand or hands on the heart gesture removes your hand from the greeting so there's no confusion about making physical contact. An added bonus is that this gesture poetically conveys warmth with a motion toward the heart.

Mitigate Virtual Fatigue and Maximize Productivity

ENGAGE

Once upon a time,
unfortunate blunders were made . . .

Tired Todd   *Frazzled Fran*   *Wearied Wanda*

LIFE AFTER LOCKDOWN

Meet three exhausted employees suffering from virtual overload:
Tired Todd, Wearied Wanda, and Frazzled Fran. Amid global
health concerns, these three shifted from working in posh high-rises

chock-full of energy and fun watercooler chats to working from home in desolate isolation. Even as many companies have returned to the office, there seems to be a noticeable shift toward a remote office/hybrid landscape, and these new environments are not without their pitfalls.

Tired Todd and Wearied Wanda are single parents with young tikes bouncing off the walls. Their office and home boundaries are haphazardly overlapping. Todd and Wanda are juggling dual roles of working and parenting. They have a new appreciation for how hamsters must feel, doing endless cardio on a wheel and getting nowhere fast.

Frazzled Fran is a mom of two junior high students who are also distance learning. She took great pride in being an avid gym rat and loved working out, but her passion for fitness fizzled in lockdown.

When Is the Work Getting Done?

Tired Todd's office is located five feet away from his bedroom, which makes for frequent flirtations with nap temptations. Wearied Wanda's computer is set up on the kitchen table, wedged between dirty dishes and her kids' art supplies. Her file cabinet is banged anytime someone opens the refrigerator. Frazzled Fran's makeshift office is her bedroom; she rolls out of bed in the morning, fixes breakfast, assigns schoolwork, then dives back under the covers, where she hunches over her laptop for a day of videoconferencing, her posture suffering. On good days, Frazzled Fran makes her bed so that she can have full access to her papers strewn over the comforter. On bad days, she sits down to dinner with the startling realization that she hasn't yet showered or brushed her teeth, since she's spent the day WFB (working from bed).

Monday, Tuesday, Blursday . . .

The weeks blur together as we ponder, "What day is it?" The typical workday leaves us physically and emotionally exhausted. More time is spent behind screens with no breaks, and less time is spent interacting with colleagues, spontaneously brainstorming in the hallway. While remote work has allowed us to master a great deal, the virtual fatigue can get to the best of us.

How do we emerge on the other side so that relationship-building persists without interruption, and virtual fatigue is mitigated during days that blend together like the endlessly repeating day Bill Murray woke up to in the film *Groundhog Day*?

GROUNDHOG DAY BLUNDERS

Where did our three bone-tired friends go wrong with allowing virtual fatigue to invade?

- **Tired Todd, Advertising Agency Executive:** Todd oversees complex ad campaigns and designs strategic marketing plans for major global clients. This kind of leadership requires him to fire on all cylinders, but his bed is too conveniently located next to his workspace, luring him into afternoon snoozes, which in turn disturb an uninterrupted night's slumber, causing him to wake each morning feeling wiped out. When Todd desperately needs to fall asleep at night, the blue light from computer screens suppresses his melatonin levels and delays sleep. Tired Todd hasn't had a fresh idea in months.

- **Wearied Wanda, Engineer Team Leader:** Wanda has ascended through the ranks at a Fortune 500 jet engine company. She performs complicated data analysis that requires laser-focused concentration. The fact that she has set up her kitchen as her makeshift workspace—also the nucleus of all crazy family commotion—isn't helping. The constant interruption of her toddlers reduces her productivity and shortens her fuse.

- **Frazzled Fran, National Sales Team Leader:** Staying on the radar of her networking circle, prospects, and clients is Fran's lifeblood for fueling her new business pipeline at her soft drink enterprise. However, since her daily schedule is now packed with videoconferencing that she doesn't initiate, the spontaneous networking she depended on to cultivate new relationships isn't happening. Her waning energy levels are due to a lack of exercise, and her new business pipeline looks bleak.

ENLIGHTEN

with Ms. Tiffany's Epiphanies®

Hello, my name is Virtual Fatigue, not to be confused with my fickle foe, Productivity. You know me well and feel my pain. Just when you think you will produce, I deplete your zest for life. Alas, amid the lockdown, you and I became bosom buddies behind the screen. As each day blurs where work and home collide,

you drift into autopilot, ending each call just to join the next.
I am the culprit hunching your shoulders, stiffening your neck,
and darkening the circles under your eyes.
I am the irritability you spew when you need to
come up for air but can't. Once you and I grow tighter,
your thinking dulls, and your ambition wanes.
Dare not be lulled into foolish belief that I am unstoppable.
I am stoppable, but you must change your ways.
Dare not deny that I am real, or I will deny you real results.

VIDEOCONFERENCING: THE FUTURE IS HERE, AND IT'S TIRING

The video call fatigue we are all experiencing is real, wreaking havoc with and slowing our productivity. Don't get me wrong—I'm not anti-videoconferencing. It's a necessary tool for remote work or connecting with offsite colleagues and customers. However, I *am* pro-productivity. We need to vary our routines to combat virtual fatigue.

Time Blocking Is Trending: Another tactic in optimizing your productivity, lowering your anxiety, and mitigating burnout is called time blocking. This is a time management technique that's not new but is experiencing a resurgence in today's quest to be more productive without the added stress. Time blocking is trending on TikTok as a slick approach to conquering your week. In essence, you schedule each minute of your workday by reserving chunks of color-coded time to accomplish a task. This allows you to prioritize your workload and visualize when to accomplish a preplanned task. Time blocking is somewhat of a glorified to-do list—but better.

It not only tells you what to do that week but when to do it and the maximum amount of time you have to devote to it. Instead of fretting about what needs to be accomplished next each day, you've already mapped out your schedule at the onset of your week.

How does time blocking relieve anxiety? Once your task is reserved visually on your calendar, you don't have to worry about it anymore. It's a way of compartmentalizing your workload in your mind so you don't have to consternate about a looming mound of upcoming work. Studies show that single-tasking improves performance and overall efficiency as opposed to trying to multitask. That's the cherry on top. Time blocking inspires you to focus on tackling one task at a time well instead of many tasks not so well. There are many time blocking apps that you can explore to download the best app for you.

NOT YOUR ORDINARY TALKING HEADS

Unnatural Eye Contact with Oversized Faces

Big talking heads in boxes staring back at you all day long requires you to be *on* in an unnatural way. As Professor Jeremy Bailenson, Stanford communications professor and founding director of the Virtual Human Interaction Lab, states:

> When someone's face is that close to ours in real life, our brains interpret it as an intense situation that is either going to lead to mating or to conflict. What's happening, in effect, when you're using [videoconferencing] for many, many hours is you're in this hyper aroused state.[10]

---

[10] Jeremy Bailenson, "Stanford Researchers Identify Four Causes for Zoom Fatigue," *Stanford News*, February 23, 2021, https://news.stanford.edu/2021/02/23/four-causes-zoom-fatigue-solutions/.

Body Language Is MIA

When full body language is impossible to read, we have to use other cues and exert more effort to appear interested and to grab the attention of others. Behind the screens, we are forced to choose our spoken words carefully. This effort coupled with intense eye contact and animated facial expressions inherent during these calls drains us. We don't have the luxury of movement to stimulate our creative thinking and problem-solving skills. We're tethered to the computer for easy access to documents. There is a plethora of nonverbal signals that are simply missed which normally would allow us to amplify our message and feed us information as to how our message is being received. This mental overload takes its toll over time.

Anxiety Contributes to Virtual Fatigue

Some are consumed with worrying about their technological skills in navigating the call, others are worried that their screen self or background are not appealing, while still others are worried about their unexpected home life disruptions. Feeling the pressure of being judged can be anxiety-inducing.

Poor Posture Poses Problems

Slouching can lead to aches and pains, headaches, and joint tension. Slouching also affects how you breathe and diminishes the ability to take those deep, cleansing breaths that feel so good.

Do you zone out and multitask during virtual meetings? Do you reread the same email multiple times without comprehension? Do you spend numerous hours on a to-do list? If so, you are a victim to a loss of focus.

To regain focus, take these **7 Prescriptions for Curing Virtual Fatigue:**

Prescription #1: Physical Boundaries. A separate, dedicated workspace is essential to manage interruptions. Every interruption breaks your focus, no matter how brief or lengthy. If you don't have the square footage for a dedicated office, invest in noise-canceling headphones to block out audible distractions. Additionally, listening to music helps to soothe and fine-tune focus, and some playlists are designed to elevate concentration. Avoid music with lyrics and stick to instrumental songs for less distraction, and make sure the source of your music isn't a phone waiting to lure you in with notifications and feeds. If you doubt your willpower, there are productivity extensions available for your web browser to block social media and other websites from distracting you.

Prescription #2: Physical Fitness. Research studies show that when your mobility is limited, so is your cognitive thinking, memory recall, comprehension, decision making, problem solving, and critical processing. When your alarm sounds, rehydrate yourself by chugging a large glass of lemon water. This small tweak to your morning routine says "Rise and Shine" like nothing else. You'll instantly feel the benefits of this transformational, healthy habit. Thereafter, jump-start your heart rate with a quick burst of exercise that energizes you. You'll invigorate yourself better with a burst of energy from exercise than you would with a cup of caffeine. I prefer doing three sets of ten burpees intertwined with ten sets of gliders first thing, but you may opt for doing push-ups, sit-ups, a wall squat, or jumping jacks. Engaging in a walking meeting will jump-start your productivity. However, this may not be possible due to lack of access to documents, child supervision, physical impairments, or weather conditions. Simply turn off your video as needed to stretch throughout the day.

Prescription #3: Posture. What happens if you try to sit with proper posture? Odds are you'll last for about forty-five seconds before immediately returning to a slouch. Practice these strategies to ensure your good posture lasts longer:

- Strengthen your core. Strengthen muscles between your shoulder blades and in your back. One session with a physical trainer or a few YouTube instructional videos can teach you how to strengthen these muscles so your posture doesn't collapse. Yoga or Pilates are also excellent ways to strengthen your core due to the controlled movements used in these classes. Currently, my favorite class is Pure Barre.

- Check your posture. Stand against a wall with the back of your feet, buttocks, palms, shoulders, and head pressing against the wall. Walk three feet forward and maintain the erect posture, then keep that same posture while sitting in a chair. Maintain muscle memory and revisit that wall from time to time to remind yourself of your ideal posture. Avoid the temptation to lean forward toward your computer, as this puts unhealthy pressure on your back. Sit all the way back. Plant your feet on the floor.

Prescription #4: Pose. Strike a pose on your video call using your most relaxed, inviting resting face. A soft smile and eye twinkles make you approachable and keep others engaged. Notify your face that you are happy to be on the call, and this will enhance your positivity.

Prescription #5: Presence. If your physical presence is compromised, you're most likely unable to breathe deeply. Before and during calls, energize yourself by practicing good breathwork. Try the 4-7-8 breathing technique: inhale for 4 seconds through your nose, hold for 7 seconds, and exhale out of your mouth for 8 seconds. Repeat five times and feel the elevation in your energy level with these deep, cleansing breaths.

Prescription #6: Pitch Bad Habits. Eliminate the following:

- Pitch distracting nonverbals. Your body movement should be smooth and slow as you engage in video, not abbreviated and jerky. Try to accentuate your points with fluid movement. Envision yourself as a conductor moving your arms to the beat of a relaxed song. Avoid spreading your fingers; keep them together or use two fingers pressed together. After you make your point, return one arm to the home base, your hip. This expansive stance allows you to sit in a resting position that consumes space and commands more authority.

- Avoid close-ups. Getting too close to the camera intrudes on the personal space of others. Pull back from the screen and reveal more of your torso so you aren't too close. Your callers will thank you for the breathing room.

Prescription #7: Power Pauses. Pausing your online and offline routine to treat yourself to a fun mental breather goes a long way toward mitigating fatigue. Our remote interactions have grown overly formalized and less spontaneous. Try these power pauses to add *oomph* to your days.

- Schedule a walking meeting or break. Meet colleagues at a park or some other serene outdoor venue. Promote the idea as a brief power-walk to which they don't need to RSVP. This boosts your internal networking efforts and refreshes the mind, body, and soul.

- Download a meditation app. My personal favorite is Headspace, but there are many calming apps that guide you through breathing exercises, playlists, and meditations; some even give you the luxury of selecting your personal favorite instructor.

- Sweat it out—it's trending. By wrapping yourself in an infrared sauna blanket, you can soothe aching muscles and relieve back pain. Some blankets even promote weight loss, glowing skin, mood elevation, and detox benefits while increasing the body's thermal energy and enhancing relaxation. My personal favorite is the HigherDOSE, but do the research to find the right one for you.

- Fake commutes. Wake up, brush your teeth, get dressed, and load your furry friend in the car. Drive in the general direction of your office, but instead stop at a local coffee shop or grab a healthy starter somewhere. Just get out of the house—and don't forget to listen to your favorite playlist and plan your achievements for that day.

- Hurried Huddles. Create opportunities to virtually collide and bump into others randomly. Invitees could be team members, an affinity group, volunteer affiliations, etc. Every two weeks, schedule a standing forty-minute video call when everyone and anyone can jump in. The first ten minutes is dedicated to Performance Praises, when everyone brags on the good work that they've noticed a colleague (or themselves) doing. During the second twenty minutes of the Hurried Huddle, the host randomly assigns breakout rooms of two people each for two to three minutes per session. Each person shows an object that reveals what makes them unique before answering a business-related question predetermined by the host. After a few minutes, another breakout room is launched to spark a new interaction with a different partner. These rapid-fire encounters continue until the twenty minutes is up. The final ten minutes of the Hurried Huddle reunites the entire group and provides an opportunity for everyone to brainstorm new ideas to enhance productivity, boost revenue, or increase efficiencies for the organization.

Screen Likeability and Leading Remote Teams with 8 Best Practices

ENLIGHTEN

with Ms. Tiffany's Epiphanies®

𝔗𝔥𝔢 𝔧𝔬 𝔠𝔬𝔪𝔪𝔞𝔫𝔡𝔪𝔢𝔫𝔱𝔰 𝔬𝔣 𝔰𝔠𝔯𝔢𝔢𝔫 𝔏𝔦𝔨𝔢𝔞𝔟𝔦𝔩𝔦𝔱𝔶

1. 𝔗𝔥𝔬𝔲 𝔰𝔥𝔞𝔩𝔱 𝔰𝔠𝔥𝔬𝔬𝔩 𝔶𝔬𝔲𝔯𝔰𝔢𝔩𝔣 𝔬𝔫 𝔱𝔥𝔢 𝔭𝔩𝔞𝔱𝔣𝔬𝔯𝔪𝔰 𝔞𝔳𝔞𝔦𝔩𝔞𝔟𝔩𝔢 𝔟𝔢𝔣𝔬𝔯𝔢 𝔞 𝔠𝔞𝔩𝔩.

Different platforms vary in features, so acquaint yourself with audience feedback and engagement tools such as polls, annotated whiteboards, breakout rooms, shared screens, video streaming, and so on. These platforms offer brief, helpful tutorials on their sites to make them user-friendly. Practice makes perfect, and it's smart to practice a call with a trusted friend who has a different Wi-Fi connection than yours.

II. Thou shalt dress to impress and be well-groomed.

> 66
>
> Your online appearance translates into your perceived performance offline.

Your online appearance translates into your perceived performance offline. Tastefully conveying expertise with a pulled-together look amid the relaxed virtual world will set you apart. Grooming yourself as though you're going into the office and dressing professionally from head to toe will motivate you to accomplish more that day. Looking polished, sharp, and put together sends a message that you care about being taken seriously.

Your virtual presence will be enhanced by wearing solid colored (not patterned) clothing with colors that complement your background. Men should be well-groomed, avoiding bushy beards and hairy necks. Well-coiffed hair looks like you put in effort and helps you to appear bright-eyed and enthused. Wearing a collared shirt projects professionalism. You can never go wrong with blazers sharply pulling together your look.

III. Thou shalt virtually look and sound your best.

Invest in professional-grade equipment beyond the technology that comes with your computer. A good-quality web camera and lapel microphone don't have to break your bank account but can make the difference in presenting a high-resolution image and not sounding like you work in a tin can. Don't forget to hardwire your internet connection using an ethernet cable to avert the surprise digital disaster of a lost Wi-Fi connection.

IV. **Thou shalt properly illuminate.**

Lighting is a critical component to get right for a video meeting. If the source of light streams from behind you, it casts dark shadows on your face, making you difficult to see, and can be perceived as being somberly unprofessional. Face a window for natural light or place a ring light or lamp in front of your computer. If you prefer softer lighting than what the ring light offers, purchase an affordable, wall-mounted light bar instead.

V. **Thou shalt properly frame yourself and engage with good eye contact.**

You wouldn't place your favorite artwork off-center and crooked in a custom frame, so why would you position yourself off-center on a video call? Center yourself and pull back from the camera so that a portion of your arms is revealed. A good measuring stick is for your computer screen to be one to one-and-a-half arm lengths away. This will allow your audience to see some of your hand gestures, which can add nice emphasis to the points that you are making. Position the camera so the lens is one to two inches above your eyeline, eliminating unpleasant reveals of your ceiling, nose hair, or double chin. Personally, I look into the lens when I'm speaking and look at the images when I am listening. Furthermore, if you designate the speaker view, not the gallery view, it enlarges whoever is speaking, which moves them closer to the lens and allows you to seem like you're peering right into their eyes. I also have some fun by placing a sticky note by the lens saying "Look here!" or a photo of my dog that draws my attention back to the lens when I drift. Looking at your lens, instead of the images, can feel awkward at first, but it engages your audience the best and becomes easier with practice.

VI. Thou shalt display a distraction-free, professional background.

On a video call, the goal is for your audience to be focused on you and your message, not distracted by your surroundings. Whether your background is real or virtual, what appears behind you should emulate a professional, real-life setting similar to what we've come to comfortably expect in the office. Virtual backgrounds take the pressure off having to tidy up your residence, and if you're self-conscious about something you don't like within your designated home space, nobody will ever know. Investing in an inexpensive green screen to showcase a first-class virtual background is definitely worth it. Stick to real-life professional settings, such as an office, conference room, or even a tasteful skyline. A classy touch is having your company logo subtly photoshopped on a virtual background to promote your branding.

VII. Thou shalt utilize nonverbal cues that amplify your message.

Move your arms and hands to artfully accentuate your message and draw your audience in. Recall Prescription #6 in the prior section and envision yourself as a musical conductor moving your arms and hands to a peaceful classical song. Conductors almost trace shapes in the air that measure each beat, but they do so in a fluid, hypnotic manner that accentuates the notes. Do the same on your video call. This visual establishes a high bar of professionalism for your delivery to be well-received.

VIII. Thou shalt make video meetings more inclusive and welcoming to All.

Since you're being mindful of what's in front of you, consider the audience on the other side of your screen. Unconscious bias can carry over to video meetings, just as it does during in-person meetings. Therefore, there's no room for meeting organizers to become tone deaf to the needs of each participant. Stay laser-focused on welcoming all participants.

Observe the following:

- **Apply the amplification strategy.** Research shows that women and people of color often feel invisible and discounted for their opinions during video calls. Former President Obama's female staffers used a strategy called *amplification* to ensure they elevated the idea of a fellow female staffer by echoing or repeating the idea and noting who originally offered it, thereby preventing another, more assertive person from stealing the credit for the idea later in the meeting. This strategy can also be employed to amplify the voices of those who are more reserved in personality and may feel overlooked.

- **Be respectful of time in scheduling meetings.** Meeting organizers should solicit from their teams the times they prefer to join video meetings. For example, during the pandemic, parents working from home were often homeschooling or assisting their children's distant learning. Additionally, meeting participants can come from different time zones, and scheduling calls too early or late in the day can interfere with personal time. The organizer should ascertain convenient blocks of time to schedule meetings and be respectful of all time zones. When scheduling meetings and sending the invite, it's courteous to use the time zone of your invitee so they don't have to translate the time zone.

- **Welcome 100% participation.** Quiet, reserved personalities may be uncomfortable interjecting in a large group. If someone gets interrupted, be the one to shine by saying, "Julie, why don't you finish your thought about XYZ? Your idea sounded interesting." The meeting organizer can also announce, "For those who haven't had an opportunity to weigh in, let's press pause here and invite you to unmute yourself and share your thoughts." If introverts are still not comfortable with a large group, create breakout rooms to send smaller groups to converse. Some people are more apt to contribute within a small group setting.

- Meeting organizers should use the hand-raising tool to encourage everyone to take turns in speaking, and the platform's poll surveys, if available, are helpful in soliciting feedback from all. Finally, distributing agendas beforehand and assigning speaking points are a great way to limit surprises and provide everyone time to prepare their contribution.

(For more, see below: Leading Remote Teams with 8 Best Practices.)

IX. Thou shalt join and leave a video meeting with professional courtesy.

If you have to exit the call early, inform your host prior to the call. Do not send a note in the chat to the host to say goodbye during the meeting. If there are several callers leaving early, the host will feel inclined to offer a polite farewell to each caller, which may fluster the host and prompt others to leave prematurely. Be courteous: Inform the host privately prior to the meeting, slip out quietly, and follow up with an email thanking them for a productive call.

x. **Thou shalt fully participate and turn your video on, when possible.**

Due to COVID-19, more people are geographically distributed and have shifted toward working remotely—a phenomenon that will be here to stay in some form or another. In turn, we must work harder to build meaningful relationships by staying on one another's radar and remaining engaged. When others see you on a video call, they feel a deeper connection since it emulates real life. A pleasant smile and nod noting agreement, a hand clapping, or even a distracted eye, a disapproving headshake, or an eye roll all make you more communicative.

> If your video is turned off, you may get overlooked.

LEADING REMOTE TEAMS WITH 8 BEST PRACTICES

1. Lead with a priority of talent retention.

As the pandemic ebbs, the workplace will bear witness to a major shift toward a blended work model. This hybrid work style offers

> Leaders need to prioritize talent retention and recognize that it's not solely about offering degrees of autonomy and control over their work/life balance.

talent a plethora of greater options in job choice, giving them much leverage. Leaders need to prioritize talent retention and recognize that it's not solely about offering degrees of autonomy and control over their work/life balance. They need to boost morale by being tuned into who is thriving, who is struggling, and who is feeling invisible so their organization survives the Great Resignation—a phenomenon occurring as the workforce quits their jobs due to a collective burnout. The U.S. workforce has never been more age-diverse, with up to five generations potentially represented in an organization at one time.

One overlooked demographic is Gen Z, whose budding careers are being launched at home, causing a loss in social connection and career fulfillment. Management must be laser-focused on bringing them into the fold and energizing this particular group. Leaders need to create opportunities for their senior team members to mentor and train their emerging leaders, whether it be through formal programs or more casual, organic gatherings. One example of a formal program that produces results is a *reciprocal mentoring program*. This not only promotes senior leaders coaching younger employees since there is real wisdom in experience, but it also inspires the younger employees to add value to the veterans' careers with their technological and/or social media savviness. The secret ingredient to making a reciprocal mentoring program successful is to realize that the pairings of mentor and mentee must organically evolve over time, not be forced through assignment. Relationships must form naturally, perhaps being cultivated at multiple social gatherings, and evolve before the mentoring process will prosper. The reciprocity element communicates a positive message that each generation has something valuable to learn from other generations.

> The reciprocity element communicates a positive message that each generation has something valuable to learn from other generations.

A surefire way to energize talent and boost retention rates could be as simple as saying thank you. These two words matter. When leaders have an attitude for gratitude, good things happen. Expressing authentic gratitude on a consistent basis (think automatic drip!) is a core value of modern business etiquette and is pivotal in energizing employees from the early career professionals to seasoned veterans. The manifestation of loyalty and productivity when we are made to feel highly valued at work is key to talent retention. And what would an etiquette book be without a nod to gratitude?

Studies show that when a leader thinks creatively about expressing gratitude, it elevates moods, energizes morale, and boosts performance. What are some creative ways to accomplish this?

- Invite a client or vendor in to express their gratitude directly to the team about what a difference they make.

- Create an online or physical "wall of gratitude" to encourage each employee to be a team player; pin public thank-you notes about colleagues when they go the extra mile.

- Send an email to upper management praising exceptional performance.

- Go old-school and write a handwritten thank-you note to the employee; that'll grab their attention like nothing else.

The more outside-the-box thinking leaders do, the bigger splash their gestures of appreciation will make in the minds of their talent when that dreaded call comes from a recruiter trying to lure them to the competition!

2. Establish clear expectations about video meetings.

Norms need to be clearly communicated by the meeting organizer. Whether it's having all videos on or explaining how to provide feedback during the call, communicate your expectations early on. Provide an overview of these expectations at the meeting's onset in the calendar invite.

3. Cultivate a high-trust hybrid culture.

Avoid micromanagement. It breaks trust. Don't fall into the trap of thinking just because your team works remotely, then that means they remotely work. If they are quiet on chat, don't panic and assume the worst. Alarmingly, a 2020 *Harvard Business Review* article revealed that "Thirty-eight percent of managers agreed that remote workers usually perform worse than those who work in an office."[11] Don't let mistrust lead to micromanagement. Let your employees'

---

[11] Sharon K. Parker, Caroline Knight, and Anita Keller, "Remote Managers Are Having Trust Issues," *Harvard Business Review,* July 30, 2020, www.hbr.org/2020/07/remote-managers-are-having-trust-issues.

results speak for themselves as to whether the work is getting done. Err on the side of robust overcommunication so they feel ownership in the future direction of the organization. A transparent leader will inspire greater team morale, loyalty, and productivity if they entrust the team with unannounced news and solicit their input.

When team members feel trusted and empowered, their full potential is tapped, and their loyalty is propelled; this gives the leader the gift of an unstoppable team.

4. Solicit straight talk and offer career path clarity.

First, an official employee engagement survey is a useful resource to figure out what's working and what's being overlooked. Make the surveys anonymous to glean all the information, especially from those who may be hesitant to speak out. Solicit input about what would make remote work better. If the surveys reveal employees need better home office equipment but there are budgetary constraints, purchase one set of equipment and use it as a reward in a contest or as an expression of gratitude for exceptional work performance.

Second, managers need to prioritize having ongoing discussions with their talent about career path clarity. Provide insight about their performance, their next role on deck, how you can help prepare them, and an estimated time frame for making it all happen. An employee's formal review should never reveal any surprises but should solely be a confirmation of prior discussions. This is a time for transparency and clarity about career path direction. It will alleviate employee anxiety and panic that they may be being overlooked.

5. Encourage the team not to do anything online that they wouldn't do in person.

A leader should verbally encourage their team to stay present with an all-hands-on-deck attitude during the entire call. Online meetings are still official meetings. Even though it's tempting to check emails, give your pet a belly rub, or watch a TV segment with your partner, you wouldn't engage in this type of multitasking in the office, so why start now? Calling team members by name throughout the call will keep everyone on their toes. However, be sensitive if you get the feeling from a participant that they cringe when they are called on directly. Respect their boundaries.

6. Schedule meetings in shorter durations and encourage breaks.

Have a frank talk with your admin about not overscheduling your calendar. Who says meetings must be scheduled back-to-back in old-school thirty- and sixty-minute time frames? These durations lead to meeting fatigue and a poor reputation of being notoriously tardy. Remember, if you're on time to a meeting, you're late, and if you're early to a meeting, you're on time. If you're late to a meeting, you're disrespecting the time of others. Introverted employees need recharging time between meetings. Introverts reset without people, and extroverts reset with people. Leaders should know their people and what energizes them. Take a breather in between calls by scheduling half-hour calls to end in twenty-five minutes and one-hour calls to end in fifty minutes. This allows you to recharge before you join your next call. Set your phone with a soft audible alert (my favorite is the harp sound) to play three minutes before the meeting's end. This politely alerts everyone that there is a hard stop coming soon and sends a message that you want to be respectful of their time and yours.

7. Encourage 100% participation for all team interaction opportunities and give employees the right tools.

Absence doesn't always make the heart grow fonder. Remote work will never replace the rich value of an IRL (in real life) office interaction. Provide your remote workers with the supplies and tools they need, such as printing accessibility, mail supplies, software programs, and office supplies. Underscore the importance of their presence whenever you schedule team interaction opportunities. Make it clear that these gatherings are not just for the newer hires. Emphasize to your seasoned employees how much of an impact they can make on the early career professionals when they show up in person. Mentoring opportunities can enhance team building and camaraderie.

8. Encourage your team to know when to eat their frogs.

- **Eat your frogs first.** Mark Twain quipped, "If it's your job to eat a frog, it's highly recommended to do it first thing in the morning. And if it's your job to eat two frogs, it's best to eat the biggest one first." This means, conquer the daunting tasks that require tedious concentration first thing in the morning when you're fresh. Have open dialogue with your remote team about this concept. Otherwise, they may procrastinate, potentially compromising their productivity. Mark Twain's advice assumes that you are at your finest first thing in the morning. However, this one-size-fits-all assumption may be outdated in light of today's flexible remote work landscape. Countless studies reveal interesting insights about morning people versus night owls, so consider numerous variances when determining if you're a morning or night person, such as age, gender, obesity level, geographic region, mental health, and whether you suffer from insomnia or sleep apnea.

- **Eat your frogs during energy bursts.** The second school of thought to discuss with team members is scheduling tougher tasks not based on time of day, but around when energy and concentration levels run the highest. Self-inventory is necessary.

Be Your Finest Virtual Communicator

ELEVATE

Learn by Doing Exercises

Self-Inventory Exercise: Reread the 7Ps for Curing Virtual Fatigue in Week 2 and the 10 Commandments of Screen Like-ability in Week 3. Write down how you plan to apply each prescription and the commandment to your work life by jotting down an actionable next step to the following:

THE 7Ps FOR CURING VIRTUAL FATIGUE

Prescription #1: Physical Boundaries

60-day Action Item _____

_____

6-month Action Item _____

_____

Prescription #2: Physical Fitness

60-day Action Item _____

_____

6-month Action Item _____

_____

Prescription #3: Posture

60-day Action Item _____

_____

6-month Action Item _____

_____

Prescription #4: Pose

60-day Action Item _____

_____

6-month Action Item _____

_____

Prescription #5: Presence

60-day Action Item _____

_____

6-month Action Item _____

_____

Prescription #6: Pitch Bad Habits

60-day Action Item _____

_____

6-month Action Item _____

_____

Prescription #7: Power Pauses

60-day Action Item _____

_____

6-month Action Item _____

_____

The 10 Commandments of Screen Likeability

I. **Thou shalt school yourself on the platforms available before a call.**

   Actionable Item: _____

   _____

   _____

II. **Thou shalt dress to impress and be well-groomed.**

   Actionable Item: _____

   _____

   _____

III. 𝕿𝖍𝖔𝖚 𝖘𝖍𝖆𝖑𝖙 𝖛𝖎𝖗𝖙𝖚𝖆𝖑𝖑𝖞 𝖑𝖔𝖔𝖐 𝖆𝖓𝖉 𝖘𝖔𝖚𝖓𝖉 𝖞𝖔𝖚𝖗 𝖇𝖊𝖘𝖙.

Actionable Item: _____

_____

_____

IV. 𝕿𝖍𝖔𝖚 𝖘𝖍𝖆𝖑𝖙 𝖕𝖗𝖔𝖕𝖊𝖗𝖑𝖞 𝖎𝖑𝖑𝖚𝖒𝖎𝖓𝖆𝖙𝖊.

Actionable Item: _____

_____

_____

V. 𝕿𝖍𝖔𝖚 𝖘𝖍𝖆𝖑𝖙 𝖕𝖗𝖔𝖕𝖊𝖗𝖑𝖞 𝖋𝖗𝖆𝖒𝖊 𝖞𝖔𝖚𝖗𝖘𝖊𝖑𝖋 𝖆𝖓𝖉 𝖊𝖓𝖌𝖆𝖌𝖊 𝖜𝖎𝖙𝖍 𝖌𝖔𝖔𝖉 𝖊𝖞𝖊 𝖈𝖔𝖓𝖙𝖆𝖈𝖙.

Actionable Item: _____

_____

_____

VI. 𝕿𝖍𝖔𝖚 𝖘𝖍𝖆𝖑𝖙 𝖉𝖎𝖘𝖕𝖑𝖆𝖞 𝖆 𝖉𝖎𝖘𝖙𝖗𝖆𝖈𝖙𝖎𝖔𝖓-𝖋𝖗𝖊𝖊, 𝖕𝖗𝖔𝖋𝖊𝖘𝖘𝖎𝖔𝖓𝖆𝖑 𝖇𝖆𝖈𝖐𝖌𝖗𝖔𝖚𝖓𝖉.

Actionable Item: _____

_____

_____

VII. Thou shalt utilize nonverbal cues that amplify your message.

Actionable Item: _____

_____

_____

VIII. Thou shalt make video meetings more inclusive and welcoming to All.

Actionable Item: _____

_____

_____

IX. Thou shalt join and leave a video meeting with professional courtesy.

Actionable Item: _____

_____

_____

X. Thou shalt fully participate and turn your video on, when possible.

Actionable Item: _____

_____

_____

Catalyzing Your Personal Brand

Identify Your Unique Value Proposition

> "Why fit in when you were born to stand out?"
>
> — DR. SEUSS

ENGAGE

Once upon a time, unfortunate blunders were made . . .

When we hear the word *branding*, our thoughts pivot to a Fortune 500 corporation spending beaucoup advertising dollars to promote its products or services. This important type of branding is known as corporate branding.

Catalyzing your own personal branding should be of equal importance because the reality is, if you don't brand yourself, someone else will. If you don't consciously cultivate your image and reputation, you risk losing control of these when others create their own impressions of you. When you take control of your own image and cultivate a uniquely authentic brand, the result is what I call your *Power Personal Brand* (PPB).

A critical aspect of shaping your PPB is ensuring it stays current. Let's take a look at the example below that underscores a blunder I could have made in my own career, but luckily I dodged this bullet.

> **If you don't brand yourself, someone else will.**

A Personal Share

After years of banking employment, I took the plunge and pursued a lifelong dream to become an entrepreneur and founder of my own training and consulting business. Engaging my network and establishing an esteemed board of advisors, I set out to join the dynamic world of entrepreneurship. My company, the Cincinnati Etiquette & Leadership Institute, LLC (CELI), empowers clients who are primarily (but not limited to) organizations seeking professional development and leadership training. CELI's website is www.etiquetteplease.com. The Cincinnati Etiquette & Leadership Institute, LLC (CELI), is proud to have earned national certification as a Women's Business Enterprise (WBE), which supports our clients' vendor diversity goals. I am the founder and a certified Business Etiquette and International Protocol Expert. I had the distinct honor of being trained and certified by the prestigious Protocol School of Washington (PSOW), the only school of its kind that is nationally accredited and recognized by the U.S. Department of Education. Simply put, PSOW is the global gold standard of training business etiquette consultants.

I am a proud second-generation PSOW alumna and was inspired to pursue this certification and found this company because of my parents' influence. They instilled in me how essential it is to help others who wish to bring out their personal excellence, inherent in all. My mom also graduated from PSOW and taught etiquette to youth, in addition to being a dedicated teacher and school administrator. My dad was a career United States Air Force fighter pilot, a colonel, and eventually the Wright-Patterson Air Force Base's comptroller in charge of the military base's finances. When you watch the movies *Top Gun* and *Top Gun: Maverick,* that was my dad, who also had the *need for speed.* He was the inspiration for my undergraduate degree and MBA in finance. Clearly, my parents had an indelible impact on the trajectory of my education, career, and personal brand. As a child, their high standards of protocol, civility, and respect were deeply ingrained in me. I observed my mom ironing my dad's undershirts, sweatpants, bed sheets, and yes, even his jeans. Everything had to be just right, leaving no room for mediocrity. When my dad walked out the door each morning in his just-shined black wingtips and pristine, pressed U.S.A.F. uniform, draped in medals of achievement, I knew he was on his way to pursue excellence and make an impressive difference in the world.

I echo Bette Midler when I say that my mom will always be "the wind beneath my wings." My mom inspired me to value etiquette and excellence for all and from all. She taught me that faith, family, respect, civility, decorum, and attention to detail mattered. I learned from her that etiquette builds confidence and credibility and puts others at ease when applied correctly. My mother's perspective, which she passed down to me, is that the whole point of etiquette is not to wag our fingers in judgment at others, but to help them feel comfortable enough in daily interactions that their highest selves can surface.

Don't Be Left in the Dust

In my mom's generation, dining etiquette was a skill set high in demand. She empowered thousands of children with dining etiquette and other soft skills for developing confidence and making favorable first impressions. However, in today's world, dining etiquette as a skill has sadly slipped in priority with the embrace of a more casual culture. I retain my conviction, however, that there is a glaring difference between knowing how to dine and knowing how to eat. However, people don't know what they don't know and may very well be unfairly judged. After dining, they might not win the deal or secure the job but will have no idea why. Therefore, it's paramount that you are in the know of the "unknown unknowns."

Fast-forward to today's fiercely competitive marketplace: It takes more than proper dining skills to have a competitive advantage. This was the tipping point when I knew I must update my mom's business model that had worked so well in a prior generation but wouldn't survive now. A new curriculum was needed so that my business and its impact would thrive and not be left in the dust.

The Branding Save

I might have been tempted to stick with the old-school way of teaching etiquette, primarily focused on dining, but was this the best branding decision to address current organizational needs and empower professionals to be the finest ambassadors of themselves they can be? Failure was not an option and staying current was a must.

I positioned my new company for success. To do this, I set

out to modernize CELI's business model, redirect my target audience, and update our training offerings. Due to my banking experience, I discovered that my sweet spot was working with the business community. To leverage my expertise and network, we shifted CELI's target client base away from school-aged youth to businesses. We also modernized the curriculum to appeal to my business clients' goals and pain points.

Since then, CELI has offered essential professional development training focused on four cornerstones: Business Etiquette and Leadership, Women's Leadership, Cultural Awareness/International Protocol, and Business Dining Etiquette.

One example of the updated curriculum is that to address the ever-evolving nature of business etiquette—a key personal branding component—we added our signature *Proper "Netiquette"* training as part of the Business Etiquette cornerstone to address stronger communication skills with email, smartphones, and social media in a professional context.

The takeaway is that when you consistently update your brand, you stay relevant, valued, and in business.

The Branding Outcome: Separating the Best from the Rest

CELI's business model is now embraced by universities and organizations, small and large, as a way to empower teams with a competitive edge in projecting professionalism, polish, and power. Our training promotes talent recruitment and retention. It's a lot less expensive to retain talent than to constantly train new talent. By continually seeking to modernize my PPB, I strive each day to be the go-to corporate etiquette thought leader who separates the best from the rest.

ENLIGHTEN

with Ms. Tiffany's Epiphanies®

CULTIVATING YOUR PERSONAL BRAND IS CRITICAL FOR UPWARD CAREER MOBILITY

> Personal branding is the purposeful shaping of an individual's reputation by promoting thought leadership or unique talents for the goal of monetization and setting oneself apart in a fiercely competitive and noisy marketplace.

Personal branding is the purposeful shaping of an individual's reputation by promoting thought leadership or unique talents for the goal of monetization and setting oneself apart in a fiercely competitive and noisy marketplace. The branding message paves the way for the individual to establish credibility so that their internal and distant networking circles expand in quality, and a greater impact is made toward career advancement.

The short and (perhaps) sweeter version of defining a personal brand is *a promise of value to the brand's stakeholders.*

Do you have a personal brand? When I pose this question, the overwhelming response is no. And that's the rub. The truth is that we all have a personal brand. Most of us aren't conscious of our personal brands, so they never get cultivated. We should all imagine ourselves as living brands. Our personal brand needs to be nurtured and consistently broadcast. Personal branding is all about dispersing data points out into the universe about what makes you essential and uniquely you.

Define Your Unique Value Proposition (UVP)

Before you can hone your personal brand, you need to identify your Unique Value Proposition (UVP). Your UVP is the impression you create in others about the singular value you consistently deliver that no one else can.

Thought-provoking questions to ask yourself in framing your UVP:

- Is there a subject matter to which you want to be perceived as a go-to expert?

- Are there character traits or personal strengths you want linked to your brand?

- What unique knowledge or passion do you possess that you could leverage to become a thought leader?

- What do others compliment you on when you aren't in the room?

- What are you better at doing than most?

4 Steps to Create Your Power Personal Brand (PPB)

Step 1: Google Yourself

You cannot shape the perceptions of others unless you learn what the world thinks of you first. Audit your online presence by first seeing if you even turn up in an internet search. Then determine if you need to clean up any dirty digital laundry. One way to do this is to have new, positive information posted online about yourself to *push down* any compromising posts a search may reveal. Strategies might include writing and posting new articles to LinkedIn or a professional blog or getting involved in community service or fundraising and providing quotes to journalists or publicists covering the organization's efforts. Anything that can get published online that places you in a positive light and highlights your unique attributes will help sharpen your online presence.

Step 2: Determine Your Unique Essence

I am a person around whom _____

_____ occurs.

Read the suggestions below then fill in the blank. The list is not all encompassing but is designed to get the creative juices flowing around the merits of your own Power Personal Brand.

Examples to help you fill in the blank:

- Creative ideas

- New business development

- Tech-savviness

- Empathy

- Positivity

- Problem solving

- Team building and collaboration

- Persuasiveness

- Brilliant conversation

- Conflict resolution

It can also be eye-opening to solicit your friends and network to fill in the blank about your unique essence.

Step 3: Associate Yourself with a Strong Brand

Create a hypothetical title for yourself to serve as an analogy for what sets you apart in your industry. You can return to this title for reference as you cultivate your personal brand. This title could be a nod to a hero, celebrity, thought leader, or a reputable company, such as "I am a trusted resource, the Google of modern business etiquette."

Other examples include:

- Martha Stewart of event planning

- Margaret Thatcher of leadership

- John Wooden of team building

- Madeleine Albright of negotiations

- Kate Middleton of poise

Step 4: Create a "Sticky Story" to Solve Problems for Others

Every miracle in life begins with a problem. The best corporate brands tell memorable, *sticky* stories about how their products or services solve problems for consumers. These stories pull at heartstrings and resonate with the brands' audiences. That same logic can apply to your personal brand. Create a sticky story about how your PPB solves problems and adds unique value to the lives of others.

Once you have created your PPB, work diligently to incorporate it into everything you do, say, and post and everything you don't do, don't say, and don't post. Remember that you must always keep modernizing the elements of your personal brand to ensure that it remains fresh and relevant in today's dynamic marketplace.

Marketing Your Business for One

ENGAGE

Once upon a time,
unfortunate blunders were made . . .

Let me introduce to you Mabel Fairweather.

Mabel was terribly embarrassed to toot her own horn and was modest to a fault. She was the kind of person that if you complimented her clothing, she would instantly launch into a litany of reasons as to why she didn't deserve the compliment. If Mabel felt mortified by accepting a simple compliment with confidence, self-promotion certainly wasn't going to come easy for her.

After working brilliantly with colleagues and producing impressive results, Mabel would divert any personal recognition by speaking in terms of *we*, never *I*. Simply put, she would deflect any admiration about her talents away from herself by magnifying the expertise of her colleagues. As a result, her achievements went largely unnoticed.

When it came time for senior management to consider bestowing promotions or leadership opportunities on her, despite Mabel's five years of stellar performance, she always touted stories of her colleagues' accomplishments. Yet again, she was passed over due to her incessant courtesy (and naivete) at cultivating everyone else's brand but neglecting to cultivate her own.

Tooting Your Own Horn Is Not a Sin

While it's admirable to shine a light on others, don't forget to shine a light on yourself. Be proud to be your own self-advocate. Generally, it's not considered bragging to promote your unique strengths. It should be thought of as a way to enlighten your corner of the world about how you can help others. Spotlighting your Unique Value Proposition benefits your employer, which in turn positions you for success, which is a win-win for everyone. Keep in mind that your competition isn't always outside the organization. Internal competition (fellow colleagues) can be just as stiff. If you don't learn to self-advocate in an articulate yet humble manner, you'll set yourself on a continuous loop to be overlooked for advancement.

ENLIGHTEN

with Ms. Tiffany's Epiphanies®

AMP UP YOUR VISIBILITY

Now that you have pinpointed your Power Personal Brand (PPB) and created a sticky story about how you solve problems, how do you create visibility so that you get noticed in a noisy, fiercely competitive marketplace? How are you going to disperse all the data points about your unique essence out into the universe for the world to do a double take?

> How you do anything says a lot about how you do everything.

To be your finest brand ambassador, three words come to mind: *promote*, *promote*, and *promote*. Imagine yourself as a living brand where perception is reality. Be strategic, consistent, and purposeful about what you share to promote your brand. Everything you do (and don't do) reflects your PPB, including how you dress and groom yourself. Even how you compose an email or respond to a conflict has a ripple effect on your brand. How you do anything says a lot about how you do everything. Every tweet, post, or share has the power to amplify or detract from your PPB.

Inspire with Insights: Become a Thought Leader

What knowledge have you acquired, skill have you attained, or passion have you ignited that empowers you to be a thought leader in your industry? Becoming an aspiring thought leader is a surefire way to promote your PPB and stay on the radar of your target audience. Thought leaders offer expertise that adds value to their clients, colleagues, and superiors. If they consistently offer their expertise with authenticity and a spirit to help, their personal brand is naturally well-received. By offering insights to help others, thought leaders build credibility that eventually develops a loyal following.

The internet has become the great equalizer for the little guy. Individuals don't have to spend a lot to promote themselves and enjoy equal access to the public as do the corporate giants. Individuals and small business owners can promote their brand by self-publishing articles or videos on LinkedIn, posting happy client testimonies, being a guest contributor on a TV news show or a podcast, or even posting videos on YouTube. The sky is the limit when deciding how to spread the word about your PPB. Remember the common golden thread that should be woven into every attempt to spread the word: Help others whenever and as much as possible.

The 5 Cs of Marketing Your Brand

1. **College:** Does your alma mater have an alumni cohort where you can network and promote your brand? Is there a university newsletter or a podcast that would value you as a guest contributor? Perhaps you could periodically author a blog post or a column touting your thought leadership?

2. **Company:** Does your company send out email blasts to clients and centers of influence that you could contribute to as a way to gain visibility? What about requesting to contribute content to your employer's website about a subject matter in which you are knowledgeable?

3. **Community:** Have you discovered a passion for a worthy charitable organization? Do you have a servant's heart for your community where your personal brand could get noticed while making a positive difference with volunteering? Your brand gains visibility with the growth of your network. Perhaps there is a young professional board that you could dip your toe into and join or an established board where you could add value and meet centers of influence.

4. **Channels:** In the wake of COVID-19, more interactions have moved online, and first impressions are now being made digitally. A strong digital brand will keep you front and center on the radars of others. It's a balancing act—avoid the temptation of going radio silent on social media and serving as a spectator to the platform's activity. Your lack of presence on social media channels could be detrimental. If you don't leverage social media, you could be viewed as irrelevant and old-school. On the other hand, watch out for posting in excess because once you've made it, you shouldn't have the spare time to post excessively. You want to create the perception that you've made it, so just wisely post.

- Select only one or two platforms to push out data points about your brand to your target audience. After you zero in on your target audience (discussed in the next section), select the social media channel that aligns with your target audience.

- **A Personal Share:** I'm obsessed with LinkedIn, which is the ideal platform to reach my network. Since my business etiquette expertise adds the most value to companies seeking professional development and leadership training, posting on Instagram or TikTok would not be the wisest choice for me.

- Finally, don't try to master too many channels. Select one or two platforms to create a strong social media presence. Generally, quality trumps quantity when it comes to your online activity.

5. **Content:** As noted above, stand out by creating your own written articles, blog posts, and digital content that solves problems and helps others. One more example is to contact your local business newspaper to offer editorials or opinion-based articles that solve common problems for others. Most people only share or comment on the content of others, so by publishing your own content, you'll stand out.

A Personal Share

When I founded CELI, I knew I had to spread the word about my new business and cultivate my own Power Personal Brand to build credibility. I worked hard on becoming a thought leader in my cottage industry to consistently add value to others' lives through helpful business etiquette and leadership advice. One day, I had an aha moment—I invited the managing editor of a regional business newspaper to coffee and convinced her to allow me to write a column in their newspaper called Ms. Tiffany's Epiphanies®. The concept I proposed was to have readers submit their questions about professional development, leadership, and business etiquette. I would answer their questions through the column as a way to uniquely help others. I became a regular guest contributor and created a loyal following. I then created a blog on my company website to house the articles. Of course, the articles were always posted on LinkedIn after they were published in the paper. By creating my own content and arranging for publicity, I offered clear value to the public, thereby exponentially elevating the awareness to my brand. In turn, that particular nurturing of my brand continues to generate new business and trust for my company.

Define Your Target Audience

ENLIGHTEN

with Ms. Tiffany's Epiphanies®

Again, the best definition of a personal brand is simple: *A promise of value to the brand's stakeholders.*

In this section, we need to define our stakeholders to whom we will promote our Power Personal Brand. A powerful brand voice won't do you much good if the wrong audience hears it. Therefore, decide who you want to influence and impress.

BE NICHE. BE BOUTIQUE.

It's wise not to try to be all things to all people. You'll appeal to no one if you try to focus on appealing to everyone. The broader your reach, the more the law of diminishing returns sets in as the financial and time costs increase. Therefore, focus on those you believe are most in need or most likely to be receptive to your offerings. You are the owner of a unique solution, so ask yourself, "Who needs my solution? Who are the stakeholders?"

The 3-Prong Approach to Identifying Your Stakeholders

1. **Direct Influencers:** Those who will pay you in wages.

   - Examples: your employer, clients, and prospects

2. **Centers of Influence:** Those who will refer you to those who will pay you in wages.

   - Examples: accountants/lawyers/financial advisors, advisory boards, charities/nonprofits, community leaders, local chamber of commerce, print and social media outlets, industry trade organizations, and delighted clients

3. **The Cheerleading Squad:** Those who encourage, support, and provide accountability—and have your back.

   - Examples: mentors, advisory boards, friends, family, and church community

Be Brief. Be Brilliant. Be Gone.

A Personal Share

One of my loyal Fortune 500 corporate clients engaged CELI's business etiquette training services for their emerging leaders. I remember this job well because it was springtime, and this client flew me to their headquarters in New York City. I had the privilege of presenting at their flagship retail store. Admittedly, I was secretly hoping to catch a glimpse of Martha Stewart herself, who was arriving the same day to set up a spring display on the first floor of this retailer's store. I vividly remember a spontaneous hallway chat with one of their top executives. The executive expressed how delighted his company was to welcome me and how evergreen and relevant he thought these timeless professional development skills are in today's world. Then he said, "Maybe you can help me, Tiffany. One of my pet peeves is walking to the elevator and running into a young professional. Our conversation usually goes something like this. I ask, 'What's happening in your corner of the world? How are you making a difference for us?' I typically receive one or two mundane responses that equally offer little value. The respondent either provides a two-hour *War and Peace* diatribe of everything they are working on, plus the kitchen sink. Or they regurgitate a twenty-second meaningless reply that pertains more to the weather forecast than their contributions."

It's imperative to be quick on your feet with describing your brand succinctly when the time comes. You need to be brief, brilliant, and gone. Attention spans are becoming painfully abbreviated. Have that fluid and effortless elevator pitch ready to explain what makes you uniquely valuable so you're memorable for future opportunities.

Your Time to Shine

ELEVATE

Learn by Doing Exercises

BRAND YOURSELF OR BE BRANDED

Start personalizing these PPB strategies to get those poignant data points about your brand out for the world to do a double take by completing these steps:

Step 1: Determine your unique essence by filling in the following blank and complete the rest of the four-step process in Part 2 of Week 1.

"I'm a person around whom _____

_____ occurs."

Step 2: Personalize the 5 Cs of Marketing Your Brand in Week 2.

Step 3: Define your target audience by creating a list of your stakeholders according to the 3-Prong Approach to Identifying Your Stakeholders in the prior section.

Step 4: Reassess your brand to keep it current and decide what needs to be updated.

Words Matter: Speak with Authority and Power Body Language

Verbal Taboos and Weak Speak to Avoid

"Once you stop learning, you start dying."

—ALBERT EINSTEIN

ENGAGE

Once upon a time, unfortunate blunders were made . . .

Words matter.

When we speak with a simplistic, elementary-level vocabulary, we diminish our powers of influence and persuasion. Consequentially, we dilute our messaging, which dilutes our impact. The goal is to project intelligence because intelligence differentiates and builds credibility.

Olivia is a woman with a new leadership role who is not being taken seriously in her workplace. Embarrassingly, she's become the brunt of office jokes regarding her chronic apologizing. But what's wrong with apologizing to keep peace? How can she command more respect?

Olivia's Blunder: Business etiquette is about self-awareness and making favorable impressions. It's about presenting yourself with savviness, power, and control using engaging communication skills. A high-caliber communication skill set allows you to be taken seriously.

However, some feel the need to be in everyone's good graces, so they needlessly apologize at every turn, thinking this will put everyone at ease. Research studies indicate that a clear gender gap prevails in that males are less inclined to say they're sorry for insignificant things. Males are more prone to take responsibility and apologize once they commit a wrongdoing. Yet men have a different measuring stick than women do about what qualifies as a wrongdoing and may not recognize when an apology is warranted. Women are socially conditioned to strive for harmony, peace, and balance, which leads to apologizing. Benita Zahn, Albany News Channel 13 anchor, stated, "Women apologize for just being . . . it's like we know we aren't really entitled to say or do something, so we preface it with an apology."

Self-restraint will help you resist the temptation to excessively apologize in order to seek validation and approval.

Canadian research cited in *The Wall Street Journal* reveals that people apologize four times a week, and on average we apologize more to strangers (22% of the time) and friends (46%) than to our own family (7%).[12] This is alarming.

What's wrong with *auto-apologizing*? It creates a perception of being inconsequential, weak, and ignorable. I'm not referring to when an apology is truly merited and responsibility should be taken. I'm talking about when people needlessly apologize for

---

[12] Elizabeth Bernstein, "I'm Very, Very, Very Sorry . . . Really?," *The Wall Street Journal*, October 18, 2010, www.wsj.com/articles/SB10001424052702304410504575560093884004442.

sending a delayed email response, bumping into a chair, leaving a meeting at a pre-peace, interrupting to ask a pertinent question, or even prerecording their voicemail messages with an apology offered at the onset for being unavailable. Really?!

How does Olivia stop the madness? First, she needs to heighten her self-awareness. She should keep a weekly record of how many times she catches herself apologizing. Moreover, she would be well-served to engage an accountability partner to help her keep track.

Second, Olivia needs to elevate the strength of her phrasing by using succinct, higher-level vocabulary.

ENLIGHTEN

with Ms. Tiffany's Epiphanies®

These contrasting replies underscore the stark differences in responding powerfully versus weakly:

WEAK RESPONSE	STRONG RESPONSE
"So sorry for my delayed response."	"Thank you for your patience with the timing of my reply."
"I'm sorry I'm not here to take your call."	"Thank you for reaching out. I'm unavailable, but your call is important to me so please leave a message."

WEAK RESPONSE	STRONG RESPONSE
"I'm sorry to bother you again."	"Sending a friendly reminder that those reports are due."
"Sorry, I interrupted you."	"Thank you for pausing. Please continue. I thought you were finished."
"Sorry, we can't purchase your product."	"Thank you for your follow-up. The timing isn't right for this year's budget."
"Sorry, but I think you're mistaken."	"Thank you for your perspective. I think that is a matter of personal opinion. However, I respect your viewpoint. If you don't mind, I would appreciate the opportunity to share mine."

Recapture respect. Don't be sorry. Exchange remorse for gratitude to speak with authority.

PESKY VERBAL TABOOS THAT
UNDERMINE CREDIBILITY

Protector Words: These are used to shield us when we don't have conviction in what we're articulating. These words reveal uncertainty coupled with a lack of competence and conviction.

1. I think

   - Example: I think I will need some advance notice.

2. Arguably

   - Example: She is arguably better at pickleball than tennis or ping-pong.

3. Actually

   - Example: I actually did read what you sent.

4. Just

   - Example: These are just my thoughts.

While We're Here: Be mindful of phraseology that excuses you from appearing knowledgeable. It could unintentionally put you in an unappealing space you don't want to live in. When someone references current events or political news, because of the divisive polarizing world we live in, it's tempting to fall back and reply, "I have no idea what's happening and can't watch the news. It makes me depressed, so I just don't watch it. I would rather listen to a relaxing podcast or catch some cat videos." This phrasing can be viewed as a cop-out, a weak excuse, or simply being uninformed.

There is a concerning threat of a growing cancel culture that has the potential of jeopardizing our freedom of speech. Just because an opinion is unpopular or doesn't sit well with society doesn't mean that society has the right to silence, bully, or cancel that person. Respectfulness and tolerance should prevail all around for everyone to feel heard and validated, not solely for those with a like-minded perspective. The trending response could also lead to a misguided perception of ignorance or insistence to bury your head in the sand and stay safe. Be careful—it's okay not to have the news on an all-day "automatic drip" of doom and gloom. However, stay informed. Know enough to be dangerous about the headlines so you can talk intelligently without appearing oblivious.

A word to the wise: See Building Block 4, Week 1: Turning Difficult Conversations into Civil Discourse for more strategies in navigating delicate topics.

Drama Words: These are unnecessary, elaborate, flowery words that insert fluff without adding much value.

1. Very; so very

   ▪ Examples: Very beautiful or very illuminating. The word *beautiful* is sufficient on its own. The word *illuminating* is sufficient with no need for the word *very* to preface it. When you add *very*, it's akin to the phrase *baby puppy*, which is unnecessary since the word *puppy* means "baby dog."

2. Totally

   ▪ Example: I totally understand your point and agree.

3. Absolutely

   ▪ Example: My boss absolutely agreed that I recruited the best candidate for the job.

Minimizer Phrases: This is language that discounts your message by seeking validation of your point. It tempts the listener to disregard your importance.

1. You probably don't remember me, but . . .
2. Does that make sense?
3. I know, right?
4. I'm not an expert on this topic, and others may disagree, but . . .
5. I know you're busy and don't have time for this, but I wanted to know . . .

Competency Phrases: These are phrases that portray doubt in your ability to successfully complete a task or undermine your mastery, expertise, aptitude, or capability to productively accomplish something.

1. I'll try my best, but no guarantees or promises.
2. That request may be beyond my pay grade.
3. I'm not sure if I'm the right person to ask, but maybe I can figure something out.
4. I'm hopeful I can do what you're asking, but I'm not sure.

While We're Here: If you're asked to take on a weighty assignment requiring experience you don't have, but the request is within your wheelhouse, say yes first and then figure out how to get it done. Too often we shy away from daunting tasks and miss the opportunity to challenge ourselves and grow. With handheld computers practically attached to our fingertips nowadays and networks chock-full of meaningful connections, step outside your comfort zone and learn something new.

Filler Words: These are meaningless words, phrases, or sounds that reveal uncertainty. They fill up pauses in speech so the speaker has more time to ponder what to say next. These verbal tics serve as annoying distractions and may scream of unpreparedness. Refer to Building Block 2, Week 2, for a deeper dive into filler words and strategies to avoid them.

1. Ya know? Or ya know what I mean?
2. Kinda
3. Like
4. Uh or um
5. Sort of
6. Like
7. Right?
8. So
9. At the end of the day
10. And whatnot

Superiority Phrases: These are smug, condescending phrases used to make the listener feel less worthy. Spoken to exaggerate oneself due to an inflated sense of self-worth, these phrases can be off-putting and patronizing. They are often used to mask the speaker's feelings of insecurity and exert dominance.

1. Again, like I have repeatedly said before . . .
2. As we already discussed . . .
3. As I mentioned earlier, obviously . . .
4. Perhaps you didn't understand this when I said it earlier.
5. Let me break it down so it's easy for you to understand.

Negative Phrases: These are responses that begin pessimistically and are often by-products of insecurity and a lack of confidence.

Negativity is prone to be habit-forming and does not project the image of competence or a can-do attitude. People are drawn to positivity, so you don't want to alienate others by speaking like a Debbie Downer or Negative Ned. When someone says thank you and you reply with "No problem," you make that person wonder if they really were being a problem in the first place. Instead, reply optimistically—just like one of my favorite restaurants. Chick-fil-A employees are trained to convey friendliness and use manners when they reply to their patrons. Their responses leave favorable last impressions, and I always walk out feeling like I was treated with the utmost respect. When people thank you, try some of these replies and watch them smile:

1. My pleasure!
2. The pleasure is all mine.
3. Of course, happy to help.
4. You are most welcome.

Furthermore, strive to answer requests by beginning with a positive. If your manager asks for your help with a project and you don't have the time, avoid replying, "No, I'm swamped and just can't fit that in." Instead say, "You know that I'm always happy to help. I'm working on two projects now, but if you would like me to table one of these that you assigned me, I would be glad to accommodate. It may postpone the completion of that assignment by two weeks."

Polished Prose: Punctuation and Grammar Matter

ENGAGE

Once upon a time,
unfortunate blunders were made . . .

In today's digital world, the internet and smartphones have radically redefined how we communicate. As noted previously, mediocrity is prevailing. Our speech is becoming casual, crass, and grammatically incorrect. Poor grammar causes us to appear lazy or uneducated. We project more intelligence when we consistently prioritize the importance of using proper grammar.

This section isn't meant to be a comprehensive English class. However, it *is* meant to heighten your self-awareness by providing shortcuts to speaking with correct grammar when using some common phrases.

Certain words are confusing because of their similarity. Outlined below are two blunders frequently and unconsciously committed.[13]

When to Use *I* and When to Use *Me*

1. Which one is correct?

   a. Liam drove Ava and I to the mall.

   b. Liam drove Ava and me to the mall.

   c. Liam drove me and Ava to the mall.

2. Which one is correct?

   a. Me and Noah attended the party.

   b. Noah and I attended the party.

   c. Noah and me attended the party.

3. Which one is correct?

   a. My friend is visiting me, Emma, and my family.

   b. My friend is visiting my family, me, and Emma.

   c. My friend is visiting Emma, my family, and me.

When to Use the Words *Good* and *Well*

Too often, we mistakenly use the word *good* when we should use *well* and vice versa. The word *good* is an adjective that modifies nouns. The word *well* is generally an adverb that modifies verbs. Therefore, learn to recognize the word you are modifying.

---

[13] Note: Answers are provided in the following Ms. Tiffany's Epiphanies®.

1. Which is proper—good or well?

   a. She presented very good/well at the corporate etiquette workshop.

   b. It's surprising that the player will feel good/well enough to play.

   c. I am doing good/well.

ENLIGHTEN

with Ms. Tiffany's Epiphanies®

Question 1
Correct Answer: b. Liam drove Ava and me to the mall.
Rule of Thumb: Remove the other person's name from the sentence, then ask yourself which sounds better, *I* or *me*. Does it sound better to say *Liam drove me to the mall* or *Liam drove I to the mall*? Therefore, you would say *Liam drove Ava and me to the mall*.

Question 2
Correct Answer: b. Noah and I attended the party.
Rule of Thumb: Per the previous rule of thumb, does it sound better to say *I attended the party* or *Me attended the party*? Of course, *I* sounds better. The fundamental principle of modern business etiquette is to stay others-focused and put the other person before yourself. This is a handy way to remember when you are struggling with whose name to put first in a sentence. Therefore, *Noah and I attended the party* is the correct answer.

Question 3

Correct Answer: c. My friend is visiting Emma, my family, and me.

Rule of Thumb: Using the previous two rules of thumb, choose *me* over *I* and put Emma and the family before yourself.

When to Use the Words Good and *Well*

1. Which is proper: *good* or *well*?

    a. She presented very good/well at the corporate etiquette workshop.

    b. It's surprising that the player will feel good/well enough to play.

    c. I am doing good/well.

The correct answers for all of the above are *well* because it modifies the verbs *presented*, *feel*, and *am doing*.

Employing proper grammar ensures that you will be taken seriously and commands respect. Care enough to speak properly so you can be the finest communicator you can be.

And one final thought: It's been proven that the more we read, the stronger our vocabulary and phraseology in our speech and writing. As Winston Churchill declared, "Nothing makes a man (person) more reverent than a library."

Power Body Language and Self-Calming Gestures to Avoid

ENLIGHTEN

with Ms. Tiffany's Epiphanies®

GENIE IN A BOTTLE

If you were granted one wish for a superpower to accelerate your career success, what would it be?

Personally, my wish would be to read the minds of others so I can better engage them. Reading minds could open doors to valuable insight as to whether the relationship is worth pursuing, how authentic a person is, and how much I need to pivot my delivery or stay the course in gaining likeability. Why is this insight important? It helps to build meaningful relationship capital, which, as previously noted, is the most critical yet often overlooked component to career success and personal fulfillment.

Clearly, humans were not created to read minds. However, if we become attuned to reading body language, it's the next best thing to being able to read another person's thoughts.

Signals to Help Accurately Read Body Language

Green Lights: Press On—You're Being Well-Received!

- **Counterfeit versus Genuine Smiles.** Two types of smiles exist: a smile expressing the glow of genuineness and a smile revealing the faux pas of fakeness. The slower the smile arrives and exits the face, the better. If a smile quickly ensues and then abruptly leaves, the authenticity of that smile is in question. If a smile remains isolated around the mouth and doesn't travel up to the eye area, then it's a polite but fake smile casting doubt. When a smile gradually forms crow's feet wrinkles around the eye area, there is true elation in a person's heart. It's the one time when wrinkles are in vogue!

- **A Nod to the Nods, Oddly Enough.** Designers preach that even numbers create balance and uniformity, while arranging items in odd numbers, such as staging a bookshelf with decorative items, creates visual appeal. Nodding during a conversation is very similar. When engaging in conversation, nod in clusters of three at opportune times. You'll notice that this simple act energizes your counterpart and invites engagement. The appropriate number of nods at just the right time expresses your keen interest and stimulates the other person. Be mindful of excessive nodding, which can convey you're wishing to impolitely rush through the exchange.

- **Fire Those Mirroring Neurons.** When your counterpart mirrors your body language and your gestures, you're on the right track.

- **A Personal Share:** I had just finished presenting at an all-day summit to a team of sales leaders on the merits of using business etiquette to boost new business. Afterward, the hiring manager approached me and inquired about CELI's other training offerings since he found the presentation valuable. Our exchange was at the end of a long day, so as I was elaborating on our wide array of curriculum, I leaned against the wall and bent my elbow to my hip. Just as I had relaxed against the wall, the hiring manager also leaned against the wall with his hand on his hip. At that moment, I knew he was on board with my message since he was mirroring my movements. Consequently, I stayed the course. Had he not mirrored my body language in some fashion, I would have searched for other body language to glean clues on whether to pivot my messaging. Can you recall a time when someone mirrored your body language? If so, they liked what you were saying.

- **Presence Is a Present.** The greatest gift a person can give is their undivided attention. If your counterpart is looking past you, checking their phone, talking *at* you instead of *with* you, you need to pivot your messaging accordingly. It may even be appropriate to politely ask if this is the best time to chat in order to heighten their self-awareness that they are zoning out. Using their name at opportune times will also call your counterpart back to you because our brains release a feel-good chemical every time we hear the sweet sound of our name. That's why it's a good practice to begin and end every call or conversation mentioning their name.

Red Lights: Stop—You're Losing Them and Need to Pivot!

- **Eye Leakage.** When you hear the word *leakage*, is it a good thing or a bad thing? It's usually bad and a definite sign of losing your audience. If the other person's gaze is not sustained and direct, you need to fix the leak. When someone doesn't maintain good eye contact while you speak, it means you're not presenting your point clearly or asking curious questions. They're confused about your message, or you're not holding their interest. It's time for agility and adjustment.

- **Crossing the Line.** When your counterpart has her arms crossed, this is a sign that she is acting out in defiance to what you're saying.

- **A Personal Share:** I was three minutes into a presentation to an audience of 250 people. When I was walking around the room striving to engage, a gentleman who had his arms crossed from the get-go caught my eye. As I earned more trust from the audience and they became highly engaged, I teased the gentleman after he had responded in an approachable manner to one of my questions. I pointed out the fact that I still had work to do to earn his trust since he must not like what I was saying. I explained that since his arms were crossed, he was hoisting a physical body barrier to my presentation. He smiled and responded that he had no idea he was doing that because that was his natural stance. He instantly broke this habit, thanked me for the heightened awareness, and eventually won my Most Valuable Participant award for being the most highly engaged attendee.

> **Be large and in charge. You convey status, authority, and power by the amount of height and space you consume.**

Furthermore, be mindful of crossing your legs to make your stature smaller. Be large and in charge. You convey status, authority, and power by the amount of height and space you consume. Crossing your legs, knee over knee, hunching your shoulders, and drawing your elbows in close to your sides can be interpreted as projecting insecurity and weakness. To project confidence, your stance should be shoulder-width apart or wider, and you should slightly lean back on your heels.

- **To Everything There Is a Season . . . Turn!** If your counterpart's feet or torso are angled away from you and not square with your body during a conversation, this is a powerful indicator that they will soon be offering a polite excuse to exit the conversation.

SELF-CALMING GESTURES TO AVOID

When your counterpart is anxious, you'll observe them unknowingly using self-soothing gestures to calm themselves. The face and neck are home to many nerve endings that, when rubbed, will lower heart rate and cortisol (the stress hormone) levels. When people are uncomfortable, they touch their faces, necks, hair, ties, necklaces, earrings, or collars to bring comfort. Look for these self-calming gestures and when you observe them, adjust your delivery, or ask them if there is a better time to connect.

Alter Your Approach When You Notice Self-Calming Gestures Like:

- Rubbing the forehead, nose, or eyes
- Stroking a moustache or beard
- Twirling or tucking one's hair or running fingers across one's hair
- Biting one's nails or lips
- Bouncing the leg
- Stroking the leg while sitting
- Wringing hands, flicking fingers, or drumming fingers on the table
- Stroking the back of the neck
- Popping gum
- Cracking knuckles
- Twisting a ring on a finger

Up-Speaking: Avoid at All Costs

I would be remiss not to mention the self-defeating habit of *up-speaking*. This is when a speaker uses a higher inflection at the end of a sentence. This creates the appearance of asking a question instead of making a definitive statement. It conveys that the speaker is uncertain in what they're communicating and needs validation. As such, this linguistic pattern signals a lack of authority, professionalism, and confidence. Be mindful to avoid it.

Test Your Nonverbal Communication

ELEVATE

Learn by Doing Exercise

How powerful is your body language? Do you project your voice well? How adept are you at being a wordsmith when you speak? Learn your Nonverbal IQ. On a scale of 1 to 10, rate yourself to determine how you score on your nonverbal cues. These cues are important to help you enhance your likeability.

Once you have your total points, go to the scale at the end of this exercise to see if your nonverbal communication tally passes the test. Revisit this exercise before you need to make any important impressions; it will serve as a poignant reminder to your key areas of refinement.

SELF-REFLECTION QUIZ FOR NONVERBAL CUES

1. BODY LANGUAGE

A. Eye Contact

Awkward	1 2 3 4 5 6 7 8 9 10	Natural and Sustained
Random	1 2 3 4 5 6 7 8 9 10	Good Mirroring
Disconnected	1 2 3 4 5 6 7 8 9 10	Engaging
Prolonged and Creepy	1 2 3 4 5 6 7 8 9 10	Natural Breaks Occurred

B. Posture

Slouching	1 2 3 4 5 6 7 8 9 10	Upright
Stiff	1 2 3 4 5 6 7 8 9 10	Relaxed
Unsettled	1 2 3 4 5 6 7 8 9 10	Comfortable, at Ease
Shrinking Stature	1 2 3 4 5 6 7 8 9 10	Expansive Stature
Breaths Rapid and Shallow	1 2 3 4 5 6 7 8 9 10	Breaths Slow and Deep
Ankle- or Knee-Wrapping	1 2 3 4 5 6 7 8 9 10	Feet Grounded, Hip-Width Apart

C. Gestures and Body Movement

Fake and Untimely	1 2 3 4 5 6 7 8 9 10	Natural and Timely
Contracted	1 2 3 4 5 6 7 8 9 10	Expansive
Fidgety	1 2 3 4 5 6 7 8 9 10	At Ease
Distracting	1 2 3 4 5 6 7 8 9 10	Composed
Random/Erratic	1 2 3 4 5 6 7 8 9 10	Purposeful
Awkward/Clumsy	1 2 3 4 5 6 7 8 9 10	Graceful

D. Facial Reactions

Dull	1 2 3 4 5 6 7 8 9 10	Animated
Fake	1 2 3 4 5 6 7 8 9 10	Genuine
Unfriendly	1 2 3 4 5 6 7 8 9 10	Friendly

2. VOICE

A. Pace

Slow or Rushed	1 2 3 4 5 6 7 8 9 10	Just Right
Annunciates Well	1 2 3 4 5 6 7 8 9 10	Slurs Words
Asked to Repeat	1 2 3 4 5 6 7 8 9 10	Clear Messaging

B. Pitch

Too High or Low	1 2 3 4 5 6 7 8 9 10	Just Right

C. Projection

Weak/Low Talking   1 2 3 4 5 6 7 8 9 10   Strong and Audible

D. Pause

Awkward Silences   1 2 3 4 5 6 7 8 9 10   Well-Timed Silences

Excessive Fillers   1 2 3 4 5 6 7 8 9 10   Minimal Verbal Fillers

3. WORDS

Slurred   1 2 3 4 5 6 7 8 9 10   Clearly Annunciated

Simple Vocabulary   1 2 3 4 5 6 7 8 9 10   High-Level Vocabulary

Casual and Crass   1 2 3 4 5 6 7 8 9 10   Formal and Polished

How did you do?

Tally up the total points.

SCORE 261–290 Bravo! You have a keen self-awareness of your nonverbal cues. You clearly understand how to successfully navigate your body language, voice, and words when communicating.

SCORE 204–260 You're doing all right, but there's room for improvement. Keep this exercise in prominent sight to serve as a friendly reminder. You got this!

SCORE 0–203 Ouch, *clutch my pearls!* Reread this Building Block and recruit an accountability partner to provide feedback on how you present yourself online and in person. You'll get there!

Proper Netiquette— Email Etiquette

Steer Clear
of Email Blunders

ENGAGE

Once upon a time,
unfortunate blunders were made . . .

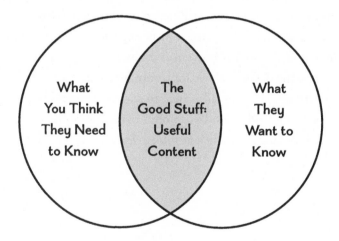

Have you noticed that communication has become casual, crass, uncaring, or uncivil? From its origination, email correspondence consumed our world over the course of about five years, and organizations are still reeling from the growing pains. Previous generations struggled with how to integrate the telegraph and telephone into their lives. In today's digital world, we're struggling with integrating email into our lives. We overuse email, misuse it, and abuse it. Reduced productivity and weakened relationship-building are the unforeseen outcomes.

If you think about it, an in-person conversation teaches patience. It unfolds slowly and requires sustained attention. We attend to its tone, warmth, dissension, personal quirks, and nuances. When we engage in sips of online communication, such as a hastily sent text, instead of gulps of real conversation, we ask simpler questions that dumb down our communication.

Alas, we've also grown accustomed to a life of constant interruption. This is underscored when we allow our inbox to become our daily to-do list. Consider the plethora of mediums available to communicate other than emailing (some of us even have multiple texting platforms). Be smart in matching the correct medium to your message. Just because email exists doesn't mean it should always be the default vehicle for communication.

That being said, email is here to stay, so learning how to be conscientious and skillful electronic communicators will prove useful. Emailing is an efficient time-saver if used correctly.

SOME BLUNDERS TO AVOID

Excellent Emails—Be Brief. Be Brilliant. Be Gone.

ENLIGHTEN

with Ms. Tiffany's Epiphanies®

Recall that in Building Block 2, Week 1, we learned that like-ability is 55% body language, 38% voice, and only 7% words. When we consider electronic delivery, we rely only on our words. Therefore, it's no wonder there is so much miscommunication and misunderstanding with emails. We only have 7% of our likeability tools to access, which means there's an alarming 93% chance of committing blunders in email correspondence.

YOUR COMPETITIVE EDGE WITH THE ELOQUENT 8

1. Remember the Holy Grail of Emailing

Whether you're an early career professional or a seasoned veteran, it's likely that the corners of your mouth instantly turn up when you hear mention of *Monty Python and the Holy Grail*. Smiles and fond memories envelop us as we recall the brilliance of this British comedy. Similarly, there's a holy grail of emailing that will keep everyone smiling.

The holy grail of emailing is to *generate fewer emails.* If you know how to construct a well-written email, the result is fewer time-sucking back-and-forth exchanges. When messages are understood out of the gate, fewer clarifying emails ensue. People appreciate the mastery to succinctly convey your point because it demonstrates a respect for their time and displays your competence. This, in turn, boosts your likeability and productivity.

> The holy grail of emailing is to generate fewer emails. If you know how to construct a well-written email, the result is fewer time-sucking back-and-forth exchanges.

2. Ask Yourself 2 Game-Changing Questions

Prior to drafting an email, organize your thoughts and frame your message by asking yourself these thought-provoking questions:

- Why am I writing?
- What do I want to be different after my email is read?

3. Use the 5 Cs of Excellent Emails

- **Be Concise:** Once you determine the reason you are writing, resist the temptation to provide unnecessary context or background. Stick to answering the questions and avoid detours. Simply tell them what time it is rather than how to build a clock. If your reader wants more information, they will ask for it.

- **Be Correct:** Project intelligence by proofreading. Be sure your message is grammatically correct with proper punctuation. Printing off your email and rereading it aloud sounds extreme but allows you to catch exponentially more mistakes.

- **Be Clear:** When your emails are crafted with clarity, there's less back-and-forth gymnastics. Use the beloved bullet point to delineate your message. Keep in mind that oftentimes your correspondent will answer your questions in the same bullet point using a different-colored font. Create new paragraphs each time a new topic is introduced. White space allows for mental breaks to ensure that your emails aren't overwhelming, which leads to your messages being read and not just skimmed. Be specific and complete. For example, when referring to a future event, specify the day of the week, the date, and the year. When referring to a time, specify a.m. or p.m. and time zone (EST, CST, etc.). State what you need and what the next steps should be.

- **Be Conversational:** One of the highest compliments you could receive is that your email made your recipient feel like you are sitting beside them having a conversation. Avoid messages that are too abrupt or too verbose. Imagine what you would say to your recipient in person and articulate your electronic message accordingly. Write like you speak. It's always mannerly to ease your reader in and out of the email with a nonbusiness pleasantry, especially if it's been a while since you've contacted them.

- **Be Courteous:** Society is suffering from an insatiable lack of civility, courtesy, and respect. More polite expressions of please, thank you, and customary manners would go a long way toward demonstrating rare professional courtesy. For example, the overuse of the reply-all feature serves as an annoying electronic disruptor to the already cluttered inboxes of those who are merely spectators of your exchanges. Also avoid being overly abrupt or crass when making a request of someone's assistance. When colleagues have worked with one another for years, a relaxed familiarity can breed toxicity in the workplace. A coworker who writes with a tone of overly relaxed familiarity wrongly assumes that the reader knows them and won't be offended by a crass message.

4. Match the Message to the Medium

How a message is delivered has a profound impact on what is being sent and your reputation. If you were mailing crystal champagne goblets to a bride and groom, would you wrap them in used, smelly newspaper? Of course not. You would package them in beautiful wedding paper with an elaborate bow secured with lots of bubble wrap. Why then would you choose to email a message that is more appropriately delivered in person or by phone so they can hear your tone? Be uniquely skilled at pairing the correct medium of delivery to your message. Perhaps it's more appropriate to deliver your message in person if persuasion skills are necessary or via text if it's time sensitive.

5. Write Emails with Military Precision and Polished Prose

Military Precision: If you're fine with your email not being read and just getting skimmed over, then don't put much thought in your subject lines. Otherwise, take note: The military has pioneered a standardized code for subject lines to quickly convey their topic and its importance. The military's brilliant practice caught my eye because my dad was a career U.S.A.F. colonel and fighter pilot who raised me with the standards of military precision. You be the judge as to whether this method is better suited at your workplace for internal or external correspondence by considering your office culture and client base.

Here are some examples of military codes for subject lines: If the recipient's signature is needed, then the subject line has the code *SIGN* and should read *SIGN: Contract.* If action is being requested from the email recipient, then the subject line should begin with the word *ACTION* and read *ACTION: RSVP Needed for Upcoming Trade Show.* If no action is required, then the word *INFO* is used in the subject as an FYI. The subject line would read *INFO: Q3 Financial Reports.* It's a welcome sight when the recipient sees that no action is required on their part—a time-saver for all.

Eye-catching subject lines alert readers and inspire action. As a result, you're taken more seriously when your emails are read and not just skimmed.

Polished Prose—Elevate Your Writing Style: A consummate writer who composes in succinct, higher-level, clear phrases earns instant trust and respect. Admittedly, stepping up your writing competence means adopting a more formal style. However, this formality doesn't have to be stuffy or condescending. A formal writing style is especially fitting at the beginning of a budding relationship (e.g., a new prospect) or while closing a deal (e.g., submitting a contract). High-caliber phraseology differentiates you as someone who deserves respect and a thoughtful response. Before you press Send, reread the email to replace simplistic, casual phrasing with bolder, livelier, higher-level phrasing. Most of us live our lives with handheld computers in our pockets. Researching a higher-level synonym for the casual word or phrase can be done in an instant.

Here are a few examples for elevating the humdrum to the compelling:

- **Ho-hum Phrase:** Thanks for meeting with me.
  - **Polished Prose:** Thank you for the privilege of your time.

- **Ho-hum Phrases:** Thanks for the opportunity. It would be great to work together.
  - **Polished Prose:** Thank you for your consideration. We take your trust seriously and look forward to the potential privilege of partnering with you.

- **Ho-hum Phrase:** We're sorry for the mistake and will get back to you about what can be done.
  - **Polished Prose:** We apologize for the inconvenience. We will get to work in making this right because you are a valued client. Is next Thursday, June 21st acceptable?

- **Ho-hum Phrase:** It was great to hear how much you like your job and company.
  - **Polished Prose:** Your enthusiasm and passion for what you do and where you work are infectious. You gave me a lot to think about with respect to x, y, and z.

6. Save Your Reputation: Are You an Electronic Elitist?

It's often not what you do but what you *don't* do that can damage your reputation. Are you broadcasting a consistent message that you are too busy or important to return emails? Is the sender not worth the effort to reply? Be careful; word gets around. Sometimes being "too busy" sends the undesirable message that you have poor time management skills, are flighty, or are self-absorbed. Rudely delaying or impolitely ignoring emails may not yield your finest moments. Here's one temperature check: Do you ask your assistant to respond to your emails or cancel your meetings when you should do it yourself? Considerate communication habits develop relationship capital, elevate reputation, boost likeability, and improve networking prowess.

The fact is, how you treat your inbox speaks volumes about your character, genuineness, professional courtesy, organizational skills, and approachability.

> ❝
> How you show up digitally says just as much about you as how you show up in person.

The Bad Boomerang of a Silent Reply: If you're unable to devote the necessary attention to responding to an email, simply say that and offer an estimated time as to when you will respond in full. Succinctly explain that you are working on a tight deadline or are traveling, but that within a set amount of time, you'll respond with the appropriate focus the sender deserves. People understand busy schedules. What they don't understand is a boomerang return of deafening silence and inaction.

7. Last Impressions Count: Your Email Closings Matter

A. When to Relax the Greeting and Closing Salutations: Do you ever grapple with the question of when to drop the greeting and closing salutation as you engage in an email thread with the same person?

Think of the email exchange emulating a real-life encounter on the street. When you bump into a friend on the sidewalk, you greet them, say their name, then speak directly to them as they respond, not repeating your greeting each time.

Consider the scenario below. Amanda and Tiffany bump into one another on a downtown sidewalk. Does their exchange sound natural?

Tiffany: Hi Amanda! I hope you are doing well. How's the family?

Amanda: Hi Tiffany! Nice to see you. We're doing great and looking forward to vacation.

Tiffany: Hi Amanda! Where are you vacationing?

Amanda: Hi Tiffany! We're going to a dude ranch near Yellowstone.

Tiffany: Hi Amanda! Wow, that sounds amazing. I love horses.

Amanda: Hi Tiffany! Me too. We can't wait for some rest and relaxation.

If the interaction above occurred in real life, nearly everyone would recognize it as awkward. You can apply that same logic to an email exchange.

Furthermore, if time has passed and the topic changes while emailing the same person, update the subject line and start fresh with the formal greeting and closing salutation. This shows professional courtesy by making it easier for your recipient to find the thread later. Think of it as though you've run into this same person on the street, just on a different day.

While We're Here: Starting a business email exchange with the word *Hey* is poor form unless you and this person are close friends. Instead use greetings such as *Hi, Hello, Good Morning,* or even just their name. Always use the person's name after the *Hi* to establish a personal rapport. Avoid the use of an exclamation mark after the person's name in the greeting, as it can be construed as overly emotional and unprofessional for business. Limit your use of the exclamation mark to one per message and save it for an expression that is more deserving of exuberance. You can still convey excitement by crafting well-worded phrasing without relying on exclamation marks.

B. Closing Salutations: Variety is the spice of life. Awkwardly signing off on your email can undermine your fluency and leave a subpar last impression. Mix it up when you close your email. The trick is to appropriately match the closing salutation with the content and tone of the message. Avoid skipping a closing altogether or defaulting to your email signature. This makes it look like you ran out of time or didn't care enough to properly close. The goal is to leave one final favorable impression by expressing an authentic closing sentiment. A common mistake is when people write or hard-code *Thanks* at the end of every email, which becomes awkward when the recipient hasn't done anything to warrant your gratitude. The closing phrase *Thanks* is overused and too casual for a business email. At the bare minimum, sign off with *Thank you*, but only if your recipient has done something to merit your gratitude.

If they haven't, use a professional closing salutation that ties into the tone and message of your email. If you are sending a formal proposal, then *Respectfully* is a nice touch. If you are apologizing for a wrongdoing, then *Sincerely* works well. If you are wishing someone well in retirement, then *All my best* resonates. If your email counterpart is a close friend and business acquaintance, then *Warm regards* or *Fondly* is fitting.

Finally, it's improper to use a sentence as a closing phrase. For example, avoid this closing mistake:

Have a great vacation,
Bob

C. Email Signature: Employers often require a standardized email signature. If not, insert a clean, uncluttered email signature that projects professionalism. Interestingly, several top business schools caution their freshmen to remove from their email signatures any hard-coded inspirational quote, political or religious affiliations, certifications, videos, and logo or anniversary images. They also advise students to delete the phrases *Sent from my iPhone* or *Please excuse typos or brevity.* Why would you want to plant a seed in the recipient's mind that you are a person prone to making mistakes or being curt? If your certifications or credentials play an important role with your job, insert a link to your LinkedIn profile to provide an uncluttered path to learn more about your qualifications.

8. Avoid Emotionally Charged Emails Like the Plague

If I showed you an email with an undertone of frustration, annoyance, or anger, chances are I can also show you a series of unfortunate events that immediately followed.

A Smart Practice: If an email has the potential to evoke negative emotion in your reader, step away from your keyboard and pick up the phone. Email should be utilized only when there is a pure exchange of facts, not as a means to hide behind a screen and say things you wouldn't have the courage to say eyeball-to-eyeball or over the phone. If you do send an emotional email, beware of hidden readers—other people you were not aware of who may be privy to the contents of your email and its tone.

Sending an Emotionally Charged Email: Meet Remorse

*Hello, my name is Remorse, not to be confused with
my Goody Two-Shoes sister, Restraint. We have not yet had the
displeasure of meeting. You may regret this particular intro.
I'm the exclamation mark punctuated in permanent ink,
not in erasable pencil. You were quick to press Send
but should have pressed Save. In drafts, I cause no harm.
All consuming, your typing fingers burn up the keyboard,
expressing your dismay. Trouble knocks at your door as
your electronic rage is unleashed. Wild horses couldn't stop
you from pressing Send. The recipient is held in scorn
to prove that you were right. Your digital flogging,
too tempting to resist. Is it better to be right and at odds,
or to be wrong and at peace? Being right may win the battle,
but a measured response wins the war.
How did your documented fury lead to career suicide,
a lost relation, or bouts of regret? Best to let it marinate.
Wait twenty-four hours while deep, cleansing breaths
refill your lungs and a good night's slumber restores your soul.
Emails should not be a refuge to house emotion,
but a safe haven for a pure exchange of facts.
Dare not bury your head in the sand in hopes I am short-lived.
Alas, I linger for long lapses of time that seem to never end.
Skip the avoidable agony and do as my self-aware sister,
Restraint, does. Hold your tongue and pocket your thumbs.
You and your career will thank me later.
You're welcome, in advance.*

The 5 Cs of Excellent Emails

ELEVATE

Learn by Doing Exercise

Below is a letter that needs editing based on the 5 Cs of Excellent Emails, explained in Week 2. Recall the 5 Cs: Be Concise; Be Correct; Be Clear; Be Conversational; Be Courteous.

In this exercise, rewrite the email to conform to the 5 Cs. For each edit you make, write in parentheses which of the 5 Cs applies to that particular edit.

For example, if there is a grammatical error in the first sentence, correct it and in parentheses insert *Be Correct*.

Hey Oliver,

I hope you are doing good. With a winter weather advisory, it hardly seems like spring . . . unless you are in Ohio. Could be far worse, as the Northeast is facing another Nor'easter.

I just wanted to follow up and let you know that I was actually able to submit the request for more balloons, and it is now waiting to go up the ranks and pending approval, so I think we are all set. I think they will be in next Monday or the following Monday.

Thanks,
Simone

Hey Oliver,

I hope you are doing ~~good~~ well **(Be Correct)**. With a winter weather advisory, it hardly seems like spring... ~~unless you are in Ohio. Could be far worse as the Northeast is facing another Nor'easter.~~ **(Be Conversational and Concise)**.

I just wanted to let you know that ~~I was actually able to~~ **(Be Concise)** submitted the request for more balloons **(Be Correct)**, and it is now waiting to go up through the ranks and pending approval so I think we are all set **(Be Concise)**. The estimated delivery date is Monday, April 2nd, or Monday, April 9th ~~I think~~ they will be in next Monday or the following Monday **(Be Clear)**.

Please let me know if I can be of any further assistance **(Be Courteous)**. Best wishes for a successful event **(Be Conversational)**.

~~Thanks,~~ Sincerely,
Simone

Closing Salutations to Impress

ELEVATE

Learn by Doing Exercise

Circle your five favorite and five least favorite phrases for a professional closing. Then check below to see if your selections match
my tried-and-tested recommendations.

- XOXO,
- Best,
- Thanks,
- Sincerely,
- Respectfully,
- Take Care,
- TTFN, (Ta-ta for now)
- Regards,
- Yours Truly,
- Warmly,

- Talk soon,
- With Appreciation,
- Thank you,
- Cordially,
- Regards,
- Best Wishes,
- Best Regards,
- Love,
- All the best,
- Cheers,

A Personal Share: Outlined below is a reveal of my favorite and
least favorite closing phrases. I developed these when providing

email etiquette services for a CEO client. He had expressed frustration that his employees did not give much thought to their email sign-offs, thus leaving poor lasting impressions. He believed that offering a thoughtless *Thanks* was not in keeping with his organization's high standards of communication.

This list of sign-offs can help close your email on a professional note. While these phrases are my favorites, the best sign-offs for you will be a matter of personal choice and writing style. Do yourself a favor by keeping your closings professional with an appropriate consideration to your message's content and tone.

Tiffany's Top 5:

1. Sincerely,

2. Best regards,

3. Thank you, (better yet, "With appreciation," or "With gratitude,")

4. Respectfully,

5. Best, (or "All the best,")

Tiffany's Bottom 5:

1. TTFN,

2. Love,

3. Regards,

4. XOXO,

5. Thanks,

Proper Netiquette— LinkedIn and Smartphone Etiquette

LinkedIn—Avoid 3 Blunders to Boost Your Online Brand

ENGAGE

Once upon a time,
unfortunate blunders were made . . .

LinkedIn Blunder #1: Photo Fails and Flat First Impressions

A questionable photo (or worse, a missing photo) on your Linked-In profile creates a subpar first impression that undermines your professionalism, credibility, and networking prowess. When photos are uploaded that don't reflect the clothing, grooming, and makeup typically worn at the office, you may not be taken seriously. Uploading an impressive headshot increases your profile views exponentially, thus enhancing your online visibility and aptness to make connections, the sought-after currency of LinkedIn.

Become familiar with the acronym APP, which spells out the three criteria advisable for uploading a professional photo: Approachability, Properness, and Professionalism. Be sure to check out the photo fails in the next section to learn how to use this new APP.

While We're on Your Profile: By creating an inclusive profile, you welcome favorable first impressions. If your name is often mispronounced, consider making it easier for others to learn by taking advantage of LinkedIn's ten-second name pronunciation audio recording feature. When others correctly address you, you put them at ease and preempt lingering guilt or awkward encounters.

It's That Easy: Tap *View Profile* then the *Edit* pencil icon in your intro card. Tap the recording button and hold to record your name. Press *Save*. A speaker icon will appear next to your name on the profile page that viewers can press to hear your name's proper pronunciation, plus any branding message you submit.

LinkedIn Blunder #2: LinkedIn Is Not a Spectator Sport

Scroll, Swipe, and Slip Out: Imagine that you arrive at a networking event, grab your nametag at the registration table, open the doors, wave to familiar faces, then spend the next two hours hunkered down in the corner on your phone, blending into the background like the wallpaper. You don't speak to a soul. You don't sip a beverage, nibble an appetizer, or join a group conversation. You don't even exchange a business card. All you do is scroll, swipe, and slip out.

Would this evening be a waste of time? Absolutely—your attendance is pointless.

Similarly, it's a waste of time to have a LinkedIn account if you're not going to actively engage. To get noticed and cultivate meaningful relationships, you have to actually do something on the platform.

LinkedIn Blunder #3: Posting without Purpose and Power

When your LinkedIn activity is purely self-promotion, what people see is an egotist or someone with too much time on their hands. Not a good look.

If you're not helping others with your content, your online activity will signal questionable character traits and get overlooked.

LinkedIn—Post with Purpose and Power

ENLIGHTEN

with Ms. Tiffany's Epiphanies®

Are you leveraging LinkedIn to its fullest potential?

LinkedIn is a powerful, feature-rich business tool that is underutilized due to a lack of understanding about how to use it. It's much more than a job search tool. Know how to embrace LinkedIn's full potential by first pinpointing your endgame.

WHAT GOALS DO YOU WANT LINKEDIN TO HELP YOU ACHIEVE?

- Highlighting your thought leadership
- Promoting your online brand
- Expanding your networking circle and earning more LinkedIn currency (i.e., connections)
- Advertising your services/products
- Discovering commonalities between you and prospects/clients/centers of influence

- Staying abreast of industry news to become a go-to expert
- Appearing on radars for new business opportunities
- Searching for jobs and spreading the word that you're open to work
- Hiring for a new position
- Other goals? _____

_____

Once you identify your primary goal(s), avoid the following blunders:

A SMART SOLVE TO BLUNDER #1, PHOTO FAILS AND FLAT FIRST IMPRESSIONS

Remove any distracting elements from your profile photo and keep it clean with a white background. Use a clear photo of your face and shoulders (not full body) to enhance your approachability. Those are the basics of effective profile photos, but here are more nuanced pitfalls to avoid:

- **The Phantom Avatar:** This is the haunting default photo that LinkedIn automatically inserts when no photo is uploaded. It looks like a ghosted silhouette. At a networking event composed of people of different experience levels, ages, and industries, I conducted an informal survey asking what types of people don't upload a LinkedIn photo. Three responses prevailed: older people who are not tech-savvy; indifferent or lazy users; and those who don't grasp the importance of having a completed Linked -In profile.

- **The Angry Arm-Crosser:** People pose with their arms crossed hoping to personify leadership. On the contrary, this body language screams *I'm angry, defensive, or closed off.*

- **The Lovebirds:** Your profile page is about you. Save the photos with your devoted partner or beloved pet for Facebook. When you secure the job interview or meet for a networking lunch after making a LinkedIn connection, will you bring your partner along too? I think not.

- **The Creepy Crop:** Attempting to crop out other people always looks unprofessional. A cropped group photo of you will often retain the disembodied body part of another person, such as someone else's hair, hand, or arm. It's awkward.

- **The Head Tilter:** When we don't hold our heads upright during business conversations or for a photo, we aren't taken as seriously. Avoid the subservient head-tilting pose.

- **The Cool Dude:** Remove distracting barriers like sunglasses, which are perfect for the beach but not for business.

- **The Fierce Full-Length:** The real estate that LinkedIn allows for a photo is limited to a tiny square box. Full-length shots make you seem less approachable, as opposed to a headshot.

- **The Drama Dresser:** Depending on your industry and position, dress appropriately. Avoid attire that is overly formal or casual. For example, avoid donning the tuxedo from your child's wedding or a T-shirt used for yard work.

There's no time like the present to invest in your online presence and upload a professional, current headshot.

A SMART SOLVE TO BLUNDER #2, LINKEDIN IS NOT A SPECTATOR SPORT

Move online connections to offline relationships. Avoid the temptation to be a LinkedIn wallflower and get involved. Why should everyone else reap the benefits of posting, publishing, messaging, liking, commenting, and connecting?

Forge Ahead with 4 Power Steps:

1. Realize That the Like, Comment, and Share Buttons Were Not All Created Equal

Be mindful that these three reactions have varying degrees of effectiveness. First, the *Like* (or *Reaction, including like, celebrate, funny, love, insightful, and curious*) button is perceived as the laziest, least effective way to engage. Your like doesn't do much but create bewilderment as to what you liked about the post. The *Thumbs Up* also leaves no opportunity for an exchange with the creator or audience. Stepping up your game means using the Comment button. That said, before commenting, read the post. There's nothing more offensive to the author than when comments reveal that you didn't read their post. Show the creator respect by offering thoughtful feedback, asking a question, or contributing an insight that promotes your own thought leadership. This opens the door for the author of the posts to like or comment on your reaction, ensuring you stay on the radar. Finally, all eyes are on the Share button. Pressing Share is the most impactful since it makes your post available to your entire network and notifies the creator of the exposure. Be sure to introduce the post by tagging people with an @mention so they will get notified. Also, add an insightful introductory sentence to your shared post. This gives you social credit.

2. Personalize Your Outreach

Avoid blending in with the masses by using LinkedIn's default invitation message. Instead, differentiate yourself by creating a personalized message to accompany your invitation to connect. Pay attention to changes in your network's profiles, status updates, anniversaries and birthdays, mutually shared connections, and postings. Send a note of congratulations or an invitation to meet in person to celebrate or catch up. For example, when a colleague or connection posts an update that they've been promoted, don't just send a default reply, or leave a generic comment such as "Congratulations." Instead, express authenticity with your own enthusiastic reply, such as "Bravo, Sharon, on this well-deserved recognition. Your strong work ethic and talents have paid off. I have no doubt that you will knock it out of the park. Let's get together soon and celebrate!"

Don't Commit the Cardinal Sin: Stop! Do not send an invitation to connect and immediately follow it with a barrage of aggressive sales pitches. This approach is a turnoff, undercutting the authenticity of your efforts to reach out and form a relationship. Do you know what I do when someone sends me a personalized invite to connect followed with an immediate flurry of salesy touchpoints? I immediately remove the thorn in my side because the trust was broken before a relationship could be cultivated. By the way, when you remove them as a connection, they do not receive notice.

3. Help Others at Every Turn

Envision your entire network holding up a "help wanted" sign and make it a priority to serve others. Sharing articles written by another or publishing your own articles demonstrates your expertise as a thought leader and sends a message that you care about offering insight to others. If you do share an article, don't merely press the Share button without a short synopsis of why the article is worth a read. Use the introductory synopsis as a window of opportunity to highlight your own thought leadership. Perhaps pull out a quote from the article to underscore the main point. Or offer to make an introduction to someone in need from your network to another person who may be helpful. Any action that helps others earns trust and builds relationship capital. A successful professional recognizes that there doesn't always have to be something in it for them.

4. Leverage the Advanced Search Filter

Generating quality prospect names for new business development efforts is where LinkedIn excels. Leverage LinkedIn's savvy advanced search filter by typing into the search bar a group you'd like to develop new business with, such as *CFOs in banking*. From there, narrow your search with filters such as location; 1st-, 2nd-, or 3rd-degree connections; or companies you are open to considering. The results will appear with populated profiles and will narrow based on qualifiers stipulated by your filters. Finish strong by clicking the new candidate's profile to see if there is a mutual connection that could provide a warm introduction. Finally, mine their profile page to identify any commonalities such as mutual schools, interests, or groups that can help you personalize your message to make more of a meaningful connection.

A SMART SOLVE TO BLUNDER #3, POSTING WITHOUT PURPOSE AND POWER

A Smart Rule of Thumb:

Dividing your posted content into thirds keeps your engagement fresh and intriguing. For example, as a corporate etiquette expert, I strive to ensure that a third of my content is geared toward helping others with corporate etiquette insight. I might post an article on post-pandemic etiquette for returning to a hybrid workplace model. Another third of my content centers on my business and any newly created workshops or curriculum (products and services). Finally, since I've offered value to others, I've earned the right to self-advocate and nurture my online brand. This can take several forms: I might post an expression of gratitude to a group of new clients who engaged CELI's training services and supported a women-owned (WBE) certified business, tout a new CELI milestone, celebrate a client endorsement, announce a recent award, or let my network know about an educational credential I've earned.

Smartphone Etiquette Rings True

ENLIGHTEN

with Ms. Tiffany's Epiphanies®

The million-dollar question you should always pose: "Which method of communication do you prefer?"

It may seem intuitive, but sadly, this question is rarely asked in business at the genesis of any new relationship. All too often, people choose the form of communication *they* are most comfortable with, giving scant thought to their counterpart's preferred method. Does the other person feel more comfortable with email? Text? A phone call instead of a Zoom meeting? You may even find that some people would rather have standing in-person meetings *(gasp!)*.

No matter what they choose, when you ask a new prospect, client, or center of influence what *their* preferred communication method is, it sets you apart. Taking the initiative underscores your interest in making their lives easier, creating value for them, and setting the tone for rare professional courtesy and consideration.

(MIS)COMMUNICATING BY SMARTPHONE

Despite their ubiquity, smartphones are still being misused in professional settings because organizations' policies have not yet evolved to offer guidance on proper mobile device behavior. Employees need—and probably want—to step up and meet this challenge. Definitive guidance from employers on how to best represent their company and themselves within and outside of the organization would be well-received. Oftentimes, smartphone users are unaware that they are annoying others or embarrassing themselves. Unfortunately, text messages can get lost in translation due to the absence of tone, body language, and nuances prevalent with in-person communication. How many hurt feelings have resulted from misunderstood texts? How much professionalism has been sacrificed with poorly conveyed texts? How many relationships have ended with emotional texts when they didn't need to end? The solution is to heighten self-awareness and self-restraint by adhering to the following rules.

Note: Be sure to read the footnotes offering greater insights to some of the commandments.

The 10 Commandments of Smartphone Use

I. Thou shalt ask permission to text someone, since it is an intimate form of communication that some believe should be reserved for social circles.

II. Thou shalt not be distracted by reading your phone under the table.[14]

---

[14] During a business meal, your phone should not be part of the place setting on the table like you see too often today. The mere presence of the phone on the table serves as a distraction. If you're expecting an important call, explain this up front to your guest, and place the phone on vibrate underneath your napkin on your lap. Excuse yourself from the table to take the call privately, then thank your guest for their understanding. Also, be mindful of smart watches pinging notifications and vying for your attention. Some people are misguided into thinking that it's okay to check their smart watches since it's not a smartphone.

III. Thou shalt convey a respectful image by using professional ringtones.

IV. Thou shalt limit quirky expressions of personality (such as exclamation marks, gifs, memes, and emojis) that could convey unprofessionalism and an undue display of emotion.

V. Thou shalt introduce oneself when texting and not assume the recipient has programmed you into their contacts.

VI. Thou shalt save texting for time-sensitive situations and be cognizant of the time of day the text is sent.[15]

VII. Thou shalt respond to texts promptly within twenty-four hours.[16]

VIII. Thou shalt remember the common courtesy of responding to texts even if it's to say that you'll respond in greater detail later.

---

[15] If the matter can wait, avoid texting, since a high percentage of texts are read within two minutes and can be viewed as intrusive. Be mindful that if you decide to put your phone in Airplane Mode or Do Not Disturb mode, a message abruptly appears that says, "Notifications have been silenced." This can be off-putting and offensive to people who may misunderstand and think you're conveying a message you don't appreciate them texting. Show courtesy by giving your texter a heads up before you toggle your phone into Airplane Mode.

[16] If another medium of communication is preferred, politely suggest the alternative medium and explain that their messages will be read in a timelier manner using the preferred medium.

ix. Thou shalt use your "indoor voice" in a professional setting and avoid distracting others by loudly talking on the phone or allowing your phone to ring incessantly.

x. Thou shalt text like one should email, but never email like some text.[17]

---

[17] When you text, do so as when you email, by using proper punctuation and grammar. Like a bad pot of coffee brewing, there's a bad texting habit brewing that may leave a bitter taste in our mouths. Punctuation is being completely omitted in texts, allowing sentences to run together. Maintain professionalism and don't say farewell to punctuation when texting for your job.

Navigate LinkedIn for Results

ELEVATE

Learn by Doing Exercise

1. Circle your top 3 goals for engaging on LinkedIn.

- Highlighting your thought leadership
- Promoting your online brand
- Expanding your networking circle and earning more LinkedIn currency (i.e., connections)
- Advertising your services/products
- Discovering commonalities between you and prospects/clients/centers of influence
- Staying abreast of industry news to become a go-to expert
- Getting on radars for new business opportunities
- Searching for jobs and spreading the word that you're open to work
- Hiring for a new position
- Other goals? _____

_____

Your engagement on LinkedIn should support the goals you have identified above.

2. Out of the 3 blunders explained in the prior section, which one resonated the most as an area for improvement in your LinkedIn engagement?

- Blunder #1: Photo Fails and Flat First Impressions

- Blunder #2: LinkedIn Is Not a Spectator Sport

- Blunder #3: Posting without Purpose and Power

3. What specific course of action(s) will you take to overcome the blunder you selected in the previous question?

_____

_____

_____

_____

The Art of Remote and In-Person Negotiations

The Skill of Powerful Persuasion

> 66
>
> "So much of life is a negotiation—even
> if you're not in business, you have
> opportunities to practice all around you."

ENGAGE

*Once upon a time,
unfortunate blunders were made . . .*

One steamy August day, feeling dejected, Storm pulled into his garage, slowly inching forward, aligning his windshield to kiss the tennis ball suspended from the ceiling. After punching in his security code, he plopped his keys into the ceramic bowl, kicked off his loafers, poured himself a cold one, turned on some Jack Johnson, and sank into the plushness of a lounge chair on his deck to watch the sunset. The burnt-orange ball of fire was sure to soothe him when it peeped through the frame of the majestic southern live oaks enveloping his deck. Storm had a passing thought: *Maybe this is the sunset that will bring new promise at dawn tomorrow.*

Storm felt discombobulated lately by the unprecedented road-blocks and rejections he encountered when he tried to persuade anyone to do anything. He usually prided himself on being a smooth operator who owned the power of persuasion, but alas, he'd lost his touch.

On the surface, the optics of Storm's life appeared perfectly under control. He was happily married with three healthy children, climbing the corporate ladder, serving as treasurer on a charitable board of directors, and selflessly caring for his aging parents. He had lifelong friends and had recently taken on the planning of a scuba-diving adventure with some buddies to Barracuda Point on Malaysia's Sipadan Island.

However, the placid surface belied a stormy sea beneath. In each segment of his life, he struggled with his powers of persuasion. For example, trust was broken when he abruptly dismissed his son's plea for a later curfew by not listening and reaching a compromise. Storm had acted out the old adage of "My house, my rules, so deal with it." Another example of a negotiation misstep was when he endangered his ascent up the corporate ladder by losing his cool with his boss rather than relying on his persuasion skills. And the list of failures continues, as we'll notice in the next section.

Discover This About Your Counterpart

ENLIGHTEN

with Ms. Tiffany's Epiphanies®

IT'S NOT ALWAYS ABOUT THE ALMIGHTY DOLLAR

Turn on your empathy radar and use discernment to pinpoint what makes your counterpart tick. Far too often, we fail at exhibiting empathy during negotiations. We don't strive to understand the pressures and pain points of our counterparts whom we are wishing to persuade. Therefore, when our negotiations become rife with an unhealthy imbalance of self-regard, we view our counterparts as those whom we want to dominate or manipulate. We all have internal drivers that spark our fight, flight, or freeze instincts. The hard work begins when you determine what motivations really drive your counterpart's behavior. Once identified, you have a clearer picture of what they need out of the negotiation, and this nugget of wisdom can serve you well in being a savvy negotiator. Padding your bank account (#3 Motivator below) isn't always the prime driver in our pursuits.

By taking the time to do a deeper dive to pinpoint what's driving a person's pursuit, you get to the crux of the matter quicker.

TOP 10 TRUE MOTIVATORS OF HUMAN BEHAVIOR

1. The need to feel valued, respected, loved, heard, validated, and/or appreciated

2. The need to feel a sense of purpose

3. The need to feel financially secure

4. The need to belong to or believe in something bigger than you

5. The need to be treated with a sense of inclusivity and equality

6. The need for autonomy, self-governance, and/or personal independence

7. The need to feel physically, emotionally, and/or spiritually safe

8. The need to feel healthy, strong, and/or in more control

9. The need to improve or preserve your reputation

10. The need to protect a loved one

Once you've pinpointed your counterpart's driving motivator, ideate concessions and compromises that will satisfy their needs while also satisfying your own.

ELEVATE

Learn by Doing Exercises

1. Bolster your negotiating prowess by examining these examples of Storm's failed negotiation efforts. This exercise will teach you how to identify true motivators. The Answer Key—based on the Top 10 True Motivators—is upside down at the end of this section.

   a. **Failed Negotiation with Boss:** In the wake of the pandemic, the balance sheet of Storm's insurance company looked dismal. Storm's boss tapped him to spearhead two companywide initiatives without additional compensation, explaining that he needed Storm to "take one for the team." Storm led a record-setting United Way fundraising campaign, coupled with revamping their intern program, all while juggling his full-time sales job. Not only was this exhausting, but it tipped his work-life balance into a deep state of imbalance that helped cause the issue with his son and, worse, his wife (see next example). Feeling taken advantage of, he stormed into his boss's office and demanded a raise. Their exchange became heated, with deep-seated resentment erupting from both sides. Unsurprisingly, his boss rejected the request and inserted a stinging reprimand in Storm's personnel file.

Which true motivator(s) did Storm overlook with his boss's negotiation? (See page 292 for list of motivators.)

_____

_____

b. **Failed Negotiation with Spouse:** Storm's wife of twenty-five years, Jackie, had high hopes of celebrating their silver wedding anniversary with a romantic getaway to the swanky Blackberry Farm Resort in Tennessee. It turned out that the only available week to get away that synced with their jobs, the kids' sports schedules, social engagements, and his mom's upcoming surgery was the week that Storm had booked a nonrefundable scuba trip with the guys. When Storm explained the dilemma to Jackie, it went over like a lead balloon, accompanied by slamming doors and a lingering silent treatment. The worst part was that he proposed going to a Florida beach for their anniversary, forgetting that Blackberry Farm had long been on Jackie's bucket list. Yikes.

Which true motivator(s) did Storm overlook with his wife's negotiation? (See page 292 for list of motivators.)

_____

_____

c. **Failed Negotiation with Son:** Now that Jake, Storm's son, had received his driver's license, he felt old enough to be trusted with a later curfew, reasoning that he was the only one of his friends who always had to call it an early night. He pleaded with his dad for a later curfew. The timing of Jake's request unfortunately fell within the same month that his high school was reeling in grief from the loss of a classmate tragically killed in a car accident. The details of the case were sparse, but parents had good cause to be apprehensive about their children getting behind the wheel of the car at a late hour. Storm, already overwhelmed by work, kept replaying the mangled-car images in his mind, fearing that the next casualty could be his own son. When Jake approached his dad for the umpteenth time, Storm snapped, "No way! Nothing good ever happens after midnight. Discussion over."

Which true motivator(s) did Storm's boss overlook when negotiating with Storm? (See page 292 for list of motivators.)

---

2. Employ your new persuasion skill of identifying true motivators and rewrite the endings of Storm's three failed negotiations to ensure more successful outcomes. At your next negotiation, be sure to identify the true motivators of your counterpart and negotiate accordingly.

Answer Key:
1. #1, #3, and #8
2. #1 and #7
3. #1, #4, #6, #8, and #9

The 8-Part Framework to Win-Win Negotiations

ENLIGHTEN

with Ms. Tiffany's Epiphanies®

> To create joint value by achieving the uppermost gain at the lowermost cost with both sides walking away feeling fairly treated and self-satisfied.

DEFINE THE NORTH STAR OF NEGOTIATIONS

Do you realize that we negotiate all day, every day, in our professional and personal lives? How you do so will determine whether or not you forge, preserve, and deepen meaningful relationships. Whether it's negotiating a contract, a real estate venture, a foreign peace agreement, a salary increase, or a curfew with your teenage son, it pays to have a strategy and tools handy.

Consider these useful principles when you enter into a negotiation, whether planned and formal or spontaneous and informal. Both parties should depart from the negotiations feeling heard, validated, and as satisfied as possible. A win-win outcome is what preserves critical relationship capital and plants seeds for additional prosperous future negotiations.

8-PART FRAMEWORK TO WIN-WIN NEGOTIATIONS

Negotiation Strategy #1: Prepare, Then Prepare More

Today's preparation guarantees tomorrow's achievements. Before the meeting, solicit your counterpart's input to collaboratively create an agenda and ground rules to follow during the negotiation. Tips include:

1. Do Your Homework

- Who should make the first offer?

- What is your bottom line?

- Where and how should both parties meet?

- Which associates should accompany you?

- Have you researched the LinkedIn profiles of your counterparts? Studied the financials? Learned their story? (Familiarize yourself with the intangibles, such as pain points and hot buttons.)

- What is your "Forget it, I'm walking away" point or monetary limit?

- Create a *Draft Agreement—Nothing in Stone* document in which both sides provide input as to what parameters need to be reached. Agree which parts of the talks are to be conducted in real life and virtually.

- If something goes awry in the future, and your counterpart is no longer employed there, what contractual assurances have you secured that will protect your deliverables?

2. Cultivate a Human Connection with Your Counterpart

- Spend time socially bonding and skip the shoptalk. If this isn't possible, arrive early to exchange nonbusiness pleasantries and discover commonalities, mutual hobbies, and shared connections. This sets a friendly tone of trust.

3. Roleplay with a Colleague

- Ask a trusted coworker to assume the role of devil's advocate to punch holes in your arguments. Embrace the constructive criticism and course-correct. Role-play how you would navigate this pushback, thinking through detours to take to avoid losing control of the talks.

4. Establish Ground Rules

- Only one person is allowed to speak at a time.

- Only one person is allowed to express anger or exasperation at a time.

- No question or idea is dumb, so condescending criticism is off-limits.

Negotiation Strategy #2: Focus on the Whys, Not the Whats

Sheila and Cliff were a married couple living their dream of owning a trendy catering business. Sheila was excited about her new gig to cater to a flock of Parrotheads (aka Jimmy Buffett fans) for a tailgate in Cincinnati, Ohio. Sheila's menu included watermelon boats, reshaping the rinds into bowl-like serving containers to hold edible goodies. Her co-owner husband was the bartender who specialized in serving up watermelon margaritas. Unfortunately, due to a hurricane in Texas, the fruit growers informed Sheila and Cliff that there was a dire watermelon shortage. They could only accommodate half their watermelon order for the Parrothead performance.

Cliff said, "No problem." As the bartender, he obviously deserved the lion's share of melons.

Sheila pounced and replied, "Not so fast." She felt she needed far more watermelons to prepare her watermelon boats.

For weeks they bickered over who should get more melons. Exasperated and further from a solution than when this started, they finally asked each other the right question starting with the word *why*.

The Problem: Sheila and Cliff had to negotiate dividing up half of their usual supply of watermelons.

The What: Maximizing the quantity of watermelons each person received.

The Why: With a newfound approach, they asked each other, "Why do you both need the watermelon so badly?" They realized that all Sheila needed were the rinds for her boatbuilding and had no use for the fruit. Cliff only desired the red fruit for his watermelon margaritas.

The Solution: Instead of dictating who should receive more watermelons, each watermelon's red fruit would first be scooped out by Cliff, and the remaining rinds would go to Sheila for her boatbuilding. Now they could get the party started.

The Lesson Learned: Focus on the whys, not the whats, of your counterpart's motivation. Ask curious questions to learn what is motivating your counterpart to feel so strongly about what they need (not what they want) out of the negotiation talks.

Negotiation Strategy #3: Keen Listening and Curious Questioning

> "Courage is what it takes to stand up and speak; courage is also what it takes to sit down and listen."

— WINSTON CHURCHILL

Active listening rewards you with valuable information in reaching a mutual agreement. Don't squander this opportunity. Knowledge is power, and the gateway to this knowledge is through open ears and closed lips. Active listening requires focus and patience as well as the restraint not to interrupt. Stop yourself from planning in your head the next words to say while your counterpart is speaking. Base your response on their prior sentences, not your preplanned agenda. The mere gesture of clarifying, "Let me repeat what I think you are saying because understanding your perspective is important to me," will be welcomed and make it easier to reason with your counterpart.

When discussions become heated, rather than becoming reactive, ask a series of curious questions to learn what's at the heart of your counterpart's resistance. Asking curious questions is also a sound stalling strategy so you can regain composure. It further equips you with wisdom to suggest viable options that may break a deadlock.

Negotiation Strategy #4: Matter Over Mind

The commonly used phrase *mind over matter* describes how will-power overcomes physical challenges. In a negotiation, the inverse is true. *Matter over mind* presents a powerful negotiation strategy that can bring two parties together in closer alliance. Leverage the physical to inspirit both sides to join together in partnership to attack the dilemma, instead of each other.

- **Where You Sit and What You Face Is Key:** At the negotiation meeting, sit side by side with your counterpart. This fosters a communal feel of partnership and cooperation against the dilemma, not face-to-face combat with each other. For example, if the problem to be solved is explained on a PowerPoint screen, sit on the same side as your counterpart, with both of you facing the screen. If the problem is detailed on a whiteboard, position the whiteboard opposite from where you both are sitting.

- **Accurately Read and Project Proper Body Language:** When reading your counterpart, look for open, expansive gestures that welcome your input such as a soft smile, uncrossed arms and legs, and the absence of nervous, self-calming gestures. If feet are pointed away from you or in a tight ankle lock, excessive nodding occurs, or your counterpart is relentlessly checking electronic devices, etc., you need to adjust your messaging because it's not being well-received. If mirroring occurs (if their nonverbal cues mimic your body language), then your messaging is well-received, so stay the course. Ensure that your body language is the winning combination of being large and in charge as well as relaxed and open-minded.

Negotiation Strategy #5: Navigate Emotions to Boost Productivity

Do you agree with this quote?

> 66
>
> "The most difficult thing in almost any negotiation is making sure that you strip it of the emotion and deal with the facts."

—HOWARD BAKER, FORMER U.S. SENATE MINORITY AND MAJORITY LEADER

- **Should Emotions Be Suppressed?** Ideally, emotions should be controlled in negotiations, not suppressed. Humans are hard-pressed to strip all emotions from interactions since emotions are hardwired into our DNA. If emotions are read accurately, they provide invaluable intelligence as to how you're being perceived. While certain emotions energize negotiations, others wreak havoc. Self-restraint allows you to flip the outcome from a combative, stressful talk to a mutual agreement. Control over your emotions in negotiations is another superpower to attain. Emotions, paired with body language and voice tone, can act as a thermometer in taking the temperature of what's

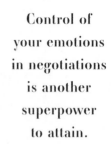

Control of your emotions in negotiations is another superpower to attain.

critical, and what's irrelevant, to your counterpart. Two questions to keep top of mind are:

- Which emotions add value to negotiations?
- How do you respond to the ugly emotions that undermine your persuasiveness?

2 Emotions That Energize Negotiations

1. **Empathy:** Are you a highly empathetic person (HEP)? If you're a HEP, you're poised for success in negotiations. Empathy is the brilliance to caringly put yourself into the shoes of another, seek to understand their perspectives and pain points, and then use this newly gleaned understanding to compassionately adjust your own thoughts and behavior toward a mutually favorable outcome. If we don't care what's important to others and what triggers them, a disconnect occurs. The highest form of empathy is when you start to get your way in the negotiations and begin asking yourself how your counterpart's sacrifices will be received by their management or impact their reputation back at their office. This is the purest form of being a HEP. If what

your counterpart is forgoing will result in a negative conse-
quence for them, trust will be broken, and nobody will win
in the long run.

2. **Positivity:** Exuding positivity is as much a smart strategy
   as it is a courtesy. When a negotiator enters the arena, a
   friendly, can-do mindset builds trust. It's imperative to
   keep communication lines open and the dialogue flowing
   to methodically work toward a resolution.

One way to exude positivity is to bring a lighthearted sense of
humor to the table, offering levity and putting everyone at ease.
Captivating, funny storytellers set themselves apart in likeability
and negotiation acumen. Like balancing on a tightrope, discern-
ing when to use humor is key. When executed correctly, this gift
energizes negotiations for wildly successful outcomes.

An indisputable way of earning trust with your counterpart
is to build a rapport before the negotiation. Create an informal
human connection by transparently sharing interests, hobbies,
dreams, worries, challenges, etc. This makes it less desirable to
attack you due to the personal bond that has formed.

Another way to exude positivity is to follow Madeleine
Albright's winning example in the art of negotiation. Among the
many lessons she taught us is that sometimes it's the more discreet
actions leaders take that can have the most profound benefit.

Ms. Albright was the first female U.S. Secretary of State, and
her persuasive prowess was unmatched. She was tough as nails
but also knew when to dial it back and kill with kindness. She
understood the power of positivity and exemplified it by leaning
into the proverb "You can catch more flies with honey than with
vinegar." As a matter of fact, Ms. Albright had a museum-like

collection of exquisite brooches, and she would select one each day to wear on her left shoulder. Before each meeting with a world leader, she selected a brooch to match the tone of the meeting. One of her prize brooches was the honeybee because of its symbolism to honey. She said that when she was trying to persuade someone in negotiations, she would wear this honeybee brooch to remind herself that her powers of persuasion were far greater by using sweetness rather than bitterness. However, it's fair to note that she also wore aggressive-style brooches when she met with a world leader who had tensions with the United States.

How do you respond to the ugly emotions that can undermine your persuasiveness?

Be mindful that people who have an aura of negative energy are powerless without your reaction. Avoid throwing gas on the fire and don't let your match be lit. Keep your reactions measured and subdued. As mentioned in Strategy #1 (preparation), enlist your counterpart's opinion in establishing ground rules that you both agree to follow. A shared project often brings dissenting parties together and demonstrates a spirit of commitment to harmonious unity.

> Be mindful that people who have an aura of negative energy are powerless without your reaction.

What are examples of ground rules to follow? One rule may be that only one person is allowed to speak at a time to prevent anyone from monopolizing the talks. Another rule may be that only one person is allowed to express anger at a time to avoid an escalation of agitation. A third rule may be to allow anyone to call for a break to cool off or even to table any further talks for another day.

Call Out Foul Play During Negotiations

Visibly display the following boundaries in the negotiation room to remind everyone to play nice in the sandbox. This practice equalizes the playing field for anyone to feel free to call a foul during the negotiation talks. If someone is feeling violated, they can point to one of the boundaries and raise a red flag. The group then redirects the discussion toward appropriateness. Outlined below are questions to serve as guardrails that provide boundaries in the pursuit of a healthy negotiation.

- Is respect being shown to all or just to a select few?

- Is one person dominating the talks? Is one person too silent and becoming invisible?

- Is anyone's authority or expertise being questioned or overexerted?

- Are opinions getting snubbed, overridden, or overlooked?

- Are untrue allegations or baseless assumptions being made?

Negotiation Strategy #6: Know when to walk away and don't give in too early

> " Let us never negotiate out of fear. But let us never fear to negotiate."

— JOHN F. KENNEDY

We have two choices when facing fear. We can either **F**ace **E**verything **A**nd **R**ise or **F**orget **E**verything **A**nd **R**un. The winning choice is the first one in negotiations. Especially with disputes, negotiators sometimes reach for the finish line too quickly. They are tempted to pull the trigger prematurely in hopes of reaching an accelerated, half-baked agreement. When dealing with a defiant personality who's convinced it's their way or the highway, some negotiators wrongly assume that if they apologize or make early concessions, this will soften hearts and guarantee amicable exchanges down the road. This wishful, unrealistic thinking often results in failed outcomes.

At the genesis of the negotiation, some feel the innate urge to be in the good graces of their counterpart. They believe that if they give in early, then the favor will surely be returned by the other person giving in later. Unfortunately, the opposite occurs. When you rush negotiations and try to win favor too early, your counterpart develops a weak and inconsequential perception of you. In fact, you set yourself up to be bullied, liberating your counterpart to dig in their heels at every turn, hoping you will cave again. Consequently, the trigger-happy apologizer loses the respect of their counterpart, and more importantly, loses their self-respect, which leads to resentment bubbling up from both sides. Be patient. Let the talks organically unfold over time before you make a sacrificial offering of your own self-respect and dignity. You'll know when the time is right to give in and accept responsibility. Your generosity of spirit will be handsomely rewarded.

A negotiator should always be ready to walk away if an impasse occurs. This captures the attention of your counterpart and garners respect, making it possible to press the reset button later.

> **Timing is everything in business, and patience to wait for the right time is tactical.**

Timing is everything in business, and patience to wait for the right time is tactical.

Negotiation Strategy #7: Optimize Options—the More, the Merrier

A Personal Share: When my husband and I travel, he dreads the stressful moment of truth at the airline check-in desk when my luggage is weighed. Admittedly, I'm not a light packer because the more options I have in outfits and shoes, the higher the odds that I'll dress correctly. I'm a big fan of maximizing my options so I have more chances to get it right.

A common mistake is to enter a negotiation with a preconceived notion that you will only accept your desired outcome. You'll garner more trust if you entertain alternative options and may even prefer a different resolution that works better for all.

A Group Think Tank

A brainstorming session can be a game changer. It invites everyone to open their minds and toss creative, yet sometimes wacky, ideas out into the universe where no judgment or criticism is allowed. Openly document each idea on a whiteboard, smartboard, or flipchart as a visual reminder that this is a cooperative effort both sides are attacking together. When the brainstorming session is completed, narrow down the plethora of ideas to a few group favorites. Keep narrowing until consensus is reached.

Negotiation Strategy #8: Stop Talking and Throw a Bone

When a sale is made, stop selling. In negotiations, when an agreement is reached, stop negotiating. The last thing you want is to unravel progress and crack the door open for second-guessing or self-doubt to creep in. As the discussions conclude, consider extending an olive branch and pacifying your counterpart with an unexpected high-value, low-cost concession or gift. This plants a seed for a favorable last impression, a seamless execution of your agreement terms, and the potential for fruitful future negotiations to occur.

Throwing your counterpart a bone could keep you out of the doghouse and make you look heroic in offering a magnanimous gesture in the spirit of goodwill. The bone doesn't have to cost a lot but might cement a lasting bond. For example, if you're working on a multimillion-dollar acquisition and have driven a hard bargain, what's the harm in suggesting that you make a significant charitable contribution to your counterpart's favorite cause? Be sure to clarify that your generosity is a one-time courtesy meant to demonstrate your genuine commitment toward cultivating a trusted, long-term relationship.

Tactics for Remote Negotiations

LEARN BY DOING

with Ms. Tiffany's Epiphanies®

Face-to-face negotiations are daunting enough, but thanks to the COVID-19 pandemic, we are bearing witness to a mass experiment of adapting to the next norm of conducting business online: remote negotiations. Instead of dreading the necessity of virtually negotiating, it's wiser to embrace the feature-rich technology of videoconferencing platforms. By dispelling myths about the challenges of virtual negotiations and learning the facts, we better equip ourselves for success when negotiating from behind a screen.

DISPEL 8 MYTHS WITH THE FACTS

Myth #1: Virtual negotiations slow down the process.

The Facts: Virtual negotiations can be successful. One compelling advantage of remote negotiations is that virtual talks are highly conducive to having more stakeholders weigh in. This can be a time-saver and a cost-cutter, since you no longer must relay what transpired during the negotiations to your team members afterward. Moreover, having more of your team present encourages collaborative buy-in and offers you support. With a greater number of internal stakeholders at the virtual table, decisions are made more quickly, and approvals are granted on the spot, which accelerates the settlement.

Myth #2: All videoconferencing platforms are created equal, so I can wing it.

The Facts: Being well-versed on the various videoconferencing platforms—such as Teams, Zoom, WebEx, etc.—makes a difference. Your counterparts may prefer different platforms so educate yourself on the ins and outs of several platforms. Although similarities exist between them, there are nuances you don't want to get mired in during a live call. The platforms' tutorials and online Q&A community are incredible resources. Kick the tires and test-drive the features by doing a practice run with a friend, cameras on. Ensure that your friend has a different Wi-Fi connection than you. Determine if you need to do a paid subscription to accommodate a particular call's needs.

Myth #3: All negotiations are best handled in person.

The Facts: The best of both worlds encompasses a hybrid arrangement of face-to-face negotiation especially for the complex issues, while using the online platform for the less complex, more routine parts of the negotiation. Collaborate with your counterpart and prepare the draft agreement, as stated above in Negotiation Strategy #1: Do Your Homework. Collectively determine which parameters should be negotiated in person and virtually.

Myth #4: Remote negotiations are exhausting.

The Facts: Scheduling shorter remote sessions instead of marathon in-person sessions will mitigate virtual fatigue. Taking frequent breaks during online negotiations will also keep attention spans laser-focused.

Myth #5: Engagement is difficult with remote negotiations.

The Facts: Video call platforms are feature-rich and leveraging them to optimize engagement and minimize distractions is easily done. If team members are geographically dispersed, take advantage of the virtual breakout rooms. This allows coworkers to vent, commiserate, or change course with a strategy during a live negotiation call.

Myth #6: Privacy is sacrificed during remote negotiations.

The Facts: Some platforms tout their security benefits more than others, so choose the one that offers you the highest comfort level. Be aware of the recording feature being turned on without your knowledge. Avoid screen-sharing your desktop to keep that information private. Before agreeing to share your screen, make sure to review the apps or documents that will appear on your desktop to preserve your privacy.

Myth #7: People look and sound awkward during virtual calls.

The Facts: Investing in a professional-grade microphone, lighting, and camera are worth it. Use the recording feature to do a self-assessment of your appearance, gestures, and idiosyncrasies. How are you positioned within the frame? What is your background revealing? What do you physically do when you're distracted or bored on a call?

Myth #8: The power of nonverbal cues is neutralized in virtual negotiations.

The Facts: You can reveal more body language to deepen the human connection online so that trust is established. Now is a good time to retake the "Test Your Nonverbal Communication" in Building Block 9, Week 4. You'll find your results will be ever-evolving, and it's smart to revisit this test occasionally.

Virtually negotiating doesn't come naturally to everyone, but this can be a learned skill that improves efficiencies for everyone the more it's practiced and perfected. In today's marketplace, people are protective and safeguard their time since it's a precious resource. They are more likely to give of their time if you create value with online negotiations. As a skilled negotiator, your task is to find solutions. You can successfully accomplish this problem-solving endeavor whether you're online or in person. It's a matter of putting yourself and your counterpart at ease online so you both can focus on the heart of the negotiation matter.

Culmination of the 12 Building Blocks and Your Next Steps

> " A bend in the road is not the end of the road unless you fail to make the turn."

—HELEN KELLER

MAKING THE TURN TO THE NEW POLISHED YOU

Alas, we've reached the finale of our learning journey, yet not your ultimate destination.

As you turn the final pages of this book or log off the laptop, you've only reached the bend in the road, not the end. Endings often precede new beginnings, and your personal journey for excellence begins now. Sheer tenacity and ambition are on the short list in presenting the new you to the world. Now comes the fun part: applying these modern business etiquette strategies to everyday life. This is the juncture where you'll begin to reap the rewards of your newly acquired skill set.

If you've invested time and reflective thought while reading this book, chances are you're a person of ambition and high standards who has an insatiable appetite to learn, grow, compete, and excel. By putting into practice these essential, yet often overlooked, professional development skills that allow your polished self to bubble to the top, your competitive edge will noticeably sparkle in the marketplace.

The spirit of this book can be encapsulated in the following 5 Tenets of Modern Business Etiquette and Leadership:

1. High-Caliber Communication Skills

2. Meaningful Relationship-Building
   (the critical ingredient to career success)

3. Authentic and Persuasive Leadership

4. An Influential Networking Circle

5. High Professionalism, Power, and Polish

MODERN BUSINESS ETIQUETTE IS A MINDSET

The skills in this book are more than a compilation of tenets, tools, and taboos. Modern business etiquette is a mindset that sets in motion your glide path to personal excellence and high distinction in today's ridiculously competitive workplace. It is an engine for personal and professional growth, not to be underestimated, but underscored.

A CURTAIN CALL AND FINAL BOW

This book's cast of characters carve out a set of scenarios that reveal what could have been if only they had read this book before they committed blunders and sent their careers into a downward spiral.

To prevent you from repeating our friends' blunders, let's engage in a thought experiment by interviewing our clumsy characters. When asked, "If you had read this book earlier, what lessons would you have learned?" we can anticipate their likely responses. Here are a few highlights of lessons learned, but certainly not an all-inclusive list:

If I Had Read This Book Earlier . . .

Bentley Fosset

Bentley laments, "If I had read this book earlier, especially **Building Block 1: Principles of Professionalism (POP!)**, I'd have known the importance of heightening one's self-awareness and self-restraint to project humility, credibility, and competence, all while earning trust as an emerging leader. **Building Block 2: Favorable First Impressions** was also eye-opening. When I arrived at my employer's orientation, I botched it by making an embarrassing spectacle of myself. We rarely receive a second chance to make a favorable first impression, and I'm living proof of it. I had my head buried so deep in the sand that I never realized how much I needed to improve my likeability because coworkers actually bristled when I approached.

"Further, my career launch could've been much smoother too, if only I had followed the guidance in **Building Block 4: Brilliant Conversation and Keen Listening.** It could have been a lifesaver when I abruptly joined a group conversation at orientation. And I wish I had read **Building Block 9: Words Matter—Speak with Authority and Power Body Language.** It outlines how to accurately read body language, particularly self-calming gestures. This is key when learning the signals of others when I'm not being well-received. I need to know when to pivot my actions and articulate myself better. The Learn by Doing exercise also would have tested the effectiveness of my nonverbal cues that often speak louder than my words."

The 7 Leaders

Larry, Lynn, Louise, Leonard, Lucy, Lydia, and Logan collectively bemoaned, "If we had read this book earlier, we would have commanded more respect and authority as leaders by familiarizing ourselves with the 7 Cs of Executive Presence, located in **Building Block 6: Executive Presence and Authentic Leadership.** The 7 Cs include:

1. Composure/Calmness

2. Connectivity

3. Curiosity

4. Charisma

5. Confidence

6. Credibility

7. Conciseness

"The Learn by Doing sections helped us understand how to apply the book's lessons. For example, the Self-Inventory Exercise revealed which of the 7 Cs of Executive Presence we should double down on and which ones we had mastered."

Jerry the Procrastinator

Jerry lamented, "If I had read this book earlier, **Building Block 5: Working a Room with a Plan and Networking for Results** would have alerted me not to wait to start networking and to realize how time sensitive networking always is. Being vigilant about knowing how to cultivate my network over time with centers of influence would have created a stronger resource for me to tap into for referrals. When the rubber hits the road and my new business development goals are right around the corner, this chapter would've been the nudge I needed to be better prepared."

Tired Todd, Wearied Wanda, and Frazzled Fran

Todd, Wanda, and Fran expressed regret, saying, "If we had read this book earlier, we could have boosted our productivity as well as our advancement opportunities by knowing how to mitigate virtual fatigue in this unprecedented hybrid work environment. **Building Block 7: Virtual Communication and the Inclusive Remote Workplace** would have energized and equipped us for this next norm and given us a clear advantage over competitors and for advancement."

Mabel Fairweather

Mabel moaned, "If I had read this book earlier, I would have been a stronger self-advocate in promoting my Personal Brand as highlighted in **Building Block 8: Catalyzing Your Personal Brand.** I'm an introvert with a more reserved personality who doesn't like to call attention to myself. This section emboldened me to comfortably promote my strengths so I could avoid the dreaded continuous loop of being overlooked for advancement. I never knew that personal branding is a survival technique for career success."

Storm

Storm lamented, "If I had read this book prior to losing my powers of persuasion in negotiations, I would not have undermined my own credibility, causing me to lose deals and weaken relationships. **Building Block 12: The Art of Remote and In-Person Negotiations**, coupled with boosting my empathy for others discussed in **Building Block 3: The Art of Meaningful Relationship-Building**, would have inspired me to put myself in the shoes of others to better understand their trigger points. Pinpointing which of the 10 True Motivators of Human Behavior drive my counterparts' behavior is key to winning negotiations, and I wish I had known."

By turning back time to 1927, **Building Block 3: The Art of Meaningful Relationship-Building** highlights the critical importance of empathy. On page 56, the true vignette of Claiborne Paul Ellis is a poignant lesson that we as a society need to heed. We must grasp how empathy carries us past prejudice and racial injustice into positive territories in our everyday lives that benefit others as much as they benefit us. Inclusive business cultures dramatically outperform those that fail this test of representation because they create and sustain higher levels of innovation due to diversity of thought and experience, workplace harmony, and the ability to achieve exceptional bottom-line results.

Tragically, research reveals that the percentage of organizations executing on the many benefits of inclusivity remain in the single digits globally. Perhaps one positive outcome of the

> **We must grasp how empathy carries us past prejudice and racial injustice into positive territories in our everyday lives that benefit others as much as they benefit us. Inclusive business cultures dramatically outperform those that fail this test of representation.**

COVID-19 pandemic will be employers' continued flexibility regarding remote work, which in turn will have a sizable impact on inclusivity. As employers offer revised policies to WFA (work from anywhere), this will attract and retain new talent that yields more diversity in the workplace. This represents a win for all.

Finally, **Building Block 10: Proper Netiquette—Email Etiquette** tackles the need to increase one's productivity and project intelligence. It's important to prevent your inbox from becoming your daily to-do list, which essentially causes you to do the work on everyone else's agenda, but not your own. Practical tips are offered about how to attain the Holy Grail in emailing: how to generate fewer emails. Matching the correct medium of communication to the message is imperative. Constructing your emails while bearing in mind the 5 Cs of Emails (Concise, Correct, Clear, Conversational, and Courteous), empowers you to project greater intelligence and competence. This section also warns that unleashing emotionally charged emails could sink one's career with reputational damage and political suicide.

Additional Resources for the Lifelong Learner

Now that you've learned the 12 Building Blocks, don't stop here. Einstein cautions that if we stop learning, we start dying, so make lifelong learning a purposeful quest throughout your career. That's what separates the good from the great leaders. Detailed below is a smart prescription offering next steps for your career ascension:

BE THE FINEST AMBASSADOR YOU CAN BE

Check out the Cincinnati Etiquette & Leadership Institute, LLC (CELI), website, www.etiquetteplease.com. A blog is available with a plethora of insightful professional development resources, such as articles as well as training offerings available via keynote speaking engagements, group workshops, and private coaching services. Discover how CELI customizes dynamic, expertly designed learning journeys that empower you to be the finest ambassador you can be for yourself, your team, and your employer. CELI is all about breathing new life into a lost art and propelling our clients to the top.

CAPSTONE BOOK QUIZ: HOW POLISHED ARE YOU WITH YOUR BUSINESS ETIQUETTE IQ?

Answer questions without peeking! Each correct answer wins you a point. Tally your total. The Answer Key is upside down on page 328.

INTRODUCTION: WHAT DOES BUSINESS ETIQUETTE HAVE TO DO WITH LEADERSHIP? EVERYTHING

1. What do research studies reveal as the worst flaw behind leaders of today?
   a. Lack of communication skills
   b. Lack of listening skills
   c. Lack of self-awareness
   d. Lack of transparency with organizational plans

BUILDING BLOCK 1: PRINCIPLES OF PROFESSIONALISM (POP!)

2. What is a strong leadership trait that involves exercising control over your tongue?
   a. Self-compassion
   b. Self-restraint
   c. Self-grace
   d. Self-indulgence

BUILDING BLOCK 2: FAVORABLE FIRST IMPRESSIONS

3. Your likeability is composed of the following percentages:
   a. 65% words, 21% voice, and 14% body language
   b. 50% words, 29% voice, and 21% body language
   c. 27% words, 33% voice, and 40% body language
   d. 7% words, 38% voice, and 55% body language

4. **Which direction do you pass the bread in distinguished dining?**

   a. Pass to the left but offer first to the person on your right

   b. Pass to the right but offer first to the person on your left

   c. Pass to the right

   d. Pass to the left

BUILDING BLOCK 3: THE ART OF MEANINGFUL RELATIONSHIP-BUILDING

5. **What percentage did empathy decline in our society in the thirty-year period starting in 1979?**

   a. 48%

   b. 32%

   c. 54%

   d. 22%

BUILDING BLOCK 4: BRILLIANT CONVERSATION AND KEEN LISTENING

6. **What is the "forgotten skill" and gateway to engaging others?**

   a. Sympathy

   b. Making favorable first and last impressions

   c. Curiosity

   d. Staying present in the moment

BUILDING BLOCK 5: WORKING A ROOM WITH A PLAN AND NETWORKING FOR RESULTS

7. **What is the universally preferred way to formally present and receive a business card?**

   a. With one hand as long as it's your left hand

b. With both hands

c. With one hand as long as it's with your right hand

d. None of the above

8. Where should you wear your name badge at a networking event?

a. High and left on your lapel/shoulder area

b. High and right on your lapel/shoulder area

c. Low and right on your lapel/shoulder area

d. On a lanyard around your neck

BUILDING BLOCK 6: EXECUTIVE PRESENCE AND AUTHENTIC LEADERSHIP

9. Which "C" is *not* included in the 7 Cs of Executive Presence?

a. Consideration

b. Credibility

c. Connectivity

d. Charisma

BUILDING BLOCK 7: VIRTUAL COMMUNICATION AND THE INCLUSIVE REMOTE WORKPLACE

10. What's the best way to look and sound during a video call?

a. Ensure that lighting is done properly with the source of light streaming from in front of you, not behind you.

b. Engage good eye contact by looking at the camera lens, not the screen images.

c. Center yourself and position computer one to one-and-a-half arm lengths away to reveal more body language.

d. All of the above

BUILDING BLOCK 8: CATALYZING YOUR PERSONAL BRAND

11. True or False?

- In personal branding, your Unique Value Proposition (UVP) is the impression you create in others about the unique value you consistently deliver that no one else can. You should be your own self-advocate and brand yourself, or someone else will.

BUILDING BLOCK 9: WORDS MATTER—SPEAK WITH AUTHORITY AND POWER BODY LANGUAGE

12. Which is proper: *good* or *well*?

- I am doing good/well.

BUILDING BLOCK 10: PROPER NETIQUETTE—EMAIL ETIQUETTE

13. What is the "Holy Grail" or most important goal of email etiquette?

- **a.** To write your emails in a way that generates fewer emails
- **b.** To write in a formal manner to project respect and intelligence
- **c.** To avoid any punctuation or grammar errors
- **d.** To send the email during business hours out of respect for the recipient

14. What are the 5 Cs of Excellent Emailing?

- **a.** Be Chatty, Be Clear, Be Connective, Be Compassionate, Be Clever
- **b.** Be Concise, Be Correct, Be Clear, Be Conversational, Be Courteous
- **c.** Be Connective, Be Concise, Be Correct, Be Clear, Be Captivating
- **d.** Be Chivalrous, Be Concise, Be Correct, Be Clear, Be Conversational

BUILDING BLOCK 11: PROPER NETIQUETTE—LINKEDIN AND SMARTPHONE ETIQUETTE

15. When reacting to a LinkedIn post, rank the preferred order of effectiveness when using the Like, Comment, and Share buttons.

   a. #1 Like, #2 Share, and #3 Comment

   b. #1 Share, #2 Like, and #3 Comment

   c. #1 Share, #2 Comment, and #3 Like

   d. #1 Comment, #2 Share, and #3 Like

BUILDING BLOCK 12—THE ART OF REMOTE AND IN-PERSON NEGOTIATIONS

16. True or False?

   - When confronted with a defiant personality during a negotiation, becoming a people pleaser early on by making concessions and/ or apologizing right away will earn trust more quickly so your counterpart will be more likely to compromise with you later.

CAPSTONE QUESTION:

17. What are the benefits of modern business etiquette?

   a. To make others comfortable so that their best selves are presented

   b. To forge meaningful relationships with authenticity and to advance with a competitive edge

   c. To employ high-caliber communication skills and project power, poise, and professionalism

   d. All of the above

HOW DID YOU DO?

(Each correct answer wins you a point. Tally your total points.)

SCORE 15–17 Impressive! You are polished and positioned for success.

SCORE 12–14 You're on your way, but there's room for improvement.

SCORE 0–11 Ouch, *clutch my pearls!* Keep working—reread *Polished* and complete the Learn by Doing exercises.

Answer Key:

1. c 2. b 3. d 4. b 5. a 6. c 7. b 8. b 9. a 10. d 11. True 12. Well 13. a 14. b 15. c 16. False 17. d

Conclusion and Encouragement to the Reader

"The world is your oyster."

— SHAKESPEARE,

THE MERRY WIVES

What do Shakespeare and oysters have to do with this book and your pursuit of a higher self? Hint: the pearl.

Excerpt from *The Merry Wives of Windsor*:

Falstaff: I will not lend thee a penny.

Pistol: Why, then, the world's mine oyster, which I with sword will open.

The character Falstaff is an overbearing, bragging, drunken knight whose comedic wit audiences of Shakespeare's time enthusiastically embraced. In the play, Falstaff refuses to lend money to Pistol, forcing Pistol to figure out on his own how to conquer the world without the critical aid of Falstaff.

In a similar manner, you are Pistol in that you are set on your quest of enlightenment, growth, and career advancement.

Of course, your degree of success depends on you and only you, rather than the good graces of some modern-day Falstaff.

This then begs the questions: How hungry are you to ascend in your career? How thirsty are you to be a lifelong learner engaged in the satisfying work of heightening your self-awareness and self-restraint?

Pistol rises to his challenge by recognizing that with the right tools, the world is his oyster. It's yours as well because you share a few common threads:

- The penny = the secret to your success
- The oyster = your career
- The sword = this book
- The pearl = the highest version of yourself

Does the oyster open easily? Absolutely not. It takes effort to pry it open, and when you do, there's no guarantee a pearl will be waiting. Furthermore, since there's no free lunch in life, it's unlikely that some Falstaff will lend you a penny to help you succeed. Hard work goes into cracking numerous shells open for just one pearl. And so, the same is true with your career success. It takes patience, practice, and perseverance, not to mention the pearls of wisdom found in this book.

As your sword, this book's learning journey will make your conquest easier. The more you apply this book's guidance and faithfully complete the exercises, the greater the probability of discovering your pearl and reaping the rewards. Each pearl of wisdom imparted in this book will make your quest for excellence that much more attainable.

And why is the pearl so special? Pearls are unique because they are the only gem shaped and found within a living creature. Similarly, you are unique and special, so don't waste time getting to work to become your polished self. The world is truly your oyster!

Letters of Dedication

LELIA CLARKE BOYD, PhD

Dear Mom,

It is with a swollen heart of deep gratitude and admiration that I dedicate this book to you, the most elegant lady I have ever had the privilege of knowing and my very best friend in life. Since I was a little girl, I've expressed a sentiment from a Bette Midler song in countless birthday and Mother's Day cards, describing you as "the wind beneath my wings." From the time you enrolled me in White Gloves and Party Manners etiquette classes at the age of 10, you sparked in me a fascination with etiquette, protocol, kindness, and respect. Later, I followed in your footsteps and became trained and certified as a second-generation graduate of the Protocol School of Washington and founded the Cincinnati Etiquette & Leadership Institute, LLC after years in the banking industry. I did this because of the premier example you set as an educator and etiquette entrepreneur. After two years of penning this manuscript and before it was published, a cavernous, aching hole was permanently ripped into my heart when you suddenly graduated to Heaven at Thanksgiving. Thanksgiving will now take on an even more profound importance since it will forever remind me of my gratitude to God for blessing me with the best mom ever. Now, you don your own set of exquisite wings as you watch over your two beloved grandsons and their future families, devoted son-in-law, adoring siblings, and me. I hear your voice daily with crisp clarity offering me wisdom, love, correction, and encouragement. I can still hear you say on dreary, rainy days, "Tiffany, you must make your own sunshine." Recently, I found in your things your handwritten note reminding yourself of these five tenets: never give up, new day–new way, believe, one more try, and persist. I am grateful when I hear your sweet voice in my ear and when I feel your presence in a dream.

You were unaware that I had planned all along to dedicate *Polished* to you, and you hadn't read a word of it because the reveal was to be a fun surprise. However, life takes unexpected twists and turns to teach us there is a higher, more divine power and plan in place in which you taught me to explicitly trust. Thank you for enlightening me that the finer things in life are not material things, but rather how we choose to project our higher selves and leave this world a little better than we found it. That should be an ongoing quest for all humans, sometimes completed and sometimes not, but we try a bit harder with each new sunrise. You led me to the three most influential persons in my life: the Father, Son, and Holy Ghost. It was exhilarating watching you be so in love with life and Christ that you made both things one. When my sweet brother, Greg, and I walked down the church aisle together as teens to accept Christ as our Savior, it was because of your love for the Lord, which revealed His unmatched love for me. You taught me the proper order for my life's priorities—God first, family second, and all else third. Now, my goal is to pay it forward by honoring your memory and legacy for etiquette and excellence. Thank you for loving me unconditionally, for forgiving me numerous times and never walking away because we are family ("blood" as you'd say), for displaying what strong work ethic looks like, for being my life's cheerleader, and for your praise and relentless support. I have no doubt that when I reread this page in the coming years, it will be tearstained, but with tears of joy, not sadness, because of the uniquely close relationship we shared. I pray *Polished* makes you proud of me because I couldn't be more proud to call you my mom. You never stopped teaching me and were never a verbal mystery when expressing yourself. No matter how stern, I always knew your advice came from a big heart and that you just wanted the best for me. You used to teasingly say, "Tiffany, you never listen to me!" Oh Mom, but I did indeed listen to you, and now I have an entire book to prove it, which emphasizes the high standards you embodied and passed along to me.

Thank you for being you. I adore your grit and grace. I adore your boundless energy of 90 years that I wish I could have bottled. As Queen Elizabeth quipped, "I have to be seen to be believed," and the same is true about you, Mom. You were one of a kind, living this life to the absolute fullest and always being a champion for family. Greg and I give a nod to your beloved Kentucky roots by raising our glasses filled with your favorite beverage, Ale-8, the only soft drink invented in Kentucky still in existence. We toast you for being tiny but mighty, thereby earning the loving nickname "Little General." You leave a beautiful "heartprint" on the souls of our family forever. Thank you for being the true inspiration to whoever reads this book and becomes better because of it.

All my love, devotion, and respect,
Tiffany

Douglas Charles Adams

Sweetheart,

I wanted to surprise you by dedicating this book to you also, the love of my life for thirty-five years and my forever soulmate. Words cannot adequately express how grateful I am for your steadfast support and wondrous encouragement as *Polished* came to life. As we both worked from home during the pandemic's quarantine, I would hole myself up in our bedroom (after you commandeered my office!) for marathon writing sessions needing an "uninterrupted bulk time of concentration." You never complained and only replied, "You do what you need to do." Stacks of research papers and scribbled notes were strewn across our bed and house for days on end. My body had grown another appendage with my computer permanently attached to my lap. Not once did you make me feel guilty for not changing out of my PJs until dinnertime, my despair for missing a workout, bowing out of a fun social outing at the last minute to meet a publishing deadline, not tidying up our room for fear of losing an important paper, or not being the most stimulating dining partner due to pure exhaustion when I could barely put my nouns and verbs together after writing all day. You were there patiently waiting to give me a fresh dose of patience, a pep talk, wise counsel, and an encouraging word to persevere. I could never have written this book without you in my corner cheering me on and believing in me.

There's a reason Mom instantly approved of you and why you two became fast friends from the get-go. She used to always say that I had a good one in you and she could leave this earth knowing her daughter would be in loving hands. When Mom graduated to Heaven, while I wrote this book, you were my rock. You helped me cope with the intense grief, took over the estate's business matters, and prepared her home for sale with painstaking sensitivity. It was a dark season of excruciating loss, but you shielded me and encouraged me to escape by writing to, hopefully, make a difference in this world. You astutely suggested I use my pain to make *Polished* even better, more relatable to my readers.

As I type this dedication, the contents of *Polished* remain unknown to you since you graciously agreed to let me present it to you after it is printed and published. I am on pins and needles in anticipation of your reaction. I hope I make you proud. Thank you for being the very best husband, devoted father, and most loving son-in-law on this planet. God blessed our family by handpicking such a loving and dedicated father, rich in integrity, principles, and spiritual values, to help parent our two beautiful boys, Blake and Brooks. We made a great team as parents, and had a lot of fun raising them. You've always said since our first year of marriage, your ultimate goal in life is to make me happy. Mission accomplished. You are my "happiness-maker" who makes my heart sing. I feel the same about you as Queen Elizabeth II felt about her Prince Philip, "My husband has quite simply been my strength and stay all these years, and I owe him a debt greater than he would ever claim." I love you oodles and boodles, bunches and bunches, lots and lots, and tons and tons!

All my love and gratitude,
Your T. Forever

Letters of Acknowledgment

Colonel Denzil H. Boyd, Jr.

Dear Daddy,

You represent the embodiment of this book's mission to strive for excellence. Although I was only given a short time to know you, those thirteen years instilled in me the courage to become a new author and to set the bar high for myself professionally and personally. You departed from this earth way too early when you suffered a heart attack at the age forty-five. Albeit brief, your life was action-packed and well lived. You demonstrated what achievement looks like and then invited me to follow your example. There's a reason why I was called "Daddy's little girl." It was because of the adoration I had for you and everything you stood for. You were a man of integrity, faith, courage, strength, and leadership. You achieved the high rank of colonel in the Air Force and were about to be promoted to general before God called you Home. You taught me to respect patriotism, protocol, power, and polish. Thank you for valiantly serving our country during your lifetime U.S.A.F. career as a fighter pilot and comptroller of Wright Patterson Air Force Base in Dayton, Ohio. I am incredibly proud of your Distinguished Flying Cross—our nation's highest pilot award for extraordinary aerial achievement. You flew over 100 combat missions, and you are my personal Top Gun hero.

I wish you could have read Polished, but you were constantly on my mind, so you were there in spirit as it was written. I can hear you say, "Tiffany, be the best." I tweaked that piece of advice to my Polished readers: "Be the best you can be." Recently, you and Mom were reunited in Heaven and it brings me great comfort that you are together again. One of your favorite sayings when Mom and you would take a romantic walk under the stars was, "Lelia, wouldn't it be a perfect night to fly?" Now, you two are flying together with the wind beneath your wings and soaring to new heights.

At a young age, I discovered the joy of writing and the awe of creation in the power of words. I will close here by sharing my love for you with my readers because I want my readers to know me. I penned this poem, which was published in the local newspaper, at the age of thirteen years:

My Dad
By Tiffany Boyd (Adams)

He lies here in his hospital bed helpless
as a bird with a broken wing.
A drab blue curtain shields him from everyone but us.
Doctors in their white smocks hover over him,
making sure the machines and tubes work right.
Telephones ring, voices murmur, and monitors beep.
The night he dies, a silvery white snow softly falls.
He leaves us as peacefully as
slow-moving ocean water leaves the shore.

Thank you, Daddy, for setting the bar high in my childhood home and for teaching that excellence, protocol, and empowerment matter.

Your little girl forever,
Tiffany

BLAKE DOUGLAS ADAMS AND BROOKS CLARKE ADAMS

Dear Blake and Brooks,

I will be forever grateful for the enthusiastic support you two gave me when I founded the Cincinnati Etiquette & Leadership Institute, LLC (CELI). The content of *Polished* is a direct correlation of what is taught at CELI. Your loving support propelled me to know that CELI's lessons would be of interest and significant value to the readers of *Polished*. You represented the voices of the younger generation by offering feedback on what would resonate and what would not. Your support took many forms, from serious discussions about curriculum to Blake sending light-hearted gifs minutes before large presentations, such as Patrick Star from SpongeBob waving a flag and cheering me on with a caption of "I'm rooting for you!" With a smile on my face and a skip in my step, you set the stage just right for me to excel. Blake repeatedly said, "It's like riding a bike, Mom. Go knock it out of the ballpark like you always do." Brooks's encouragement came in the uplifting form of advice to think positively and to believe in myself, which was key.

I am honored that you two were handpicked by God to be part of our close-knit family. We proudly raised you boys with the deepest of unconditional love in our hearts and equipped you with a strong moral compass. During your childhood, there was a reason why my nickname for Blake was "Sunshine." He truly lights up a room when he enters it and lit up our world when he was born. With an uncanny resemblance to his Uncle Greg's handsome smile, Blake's smile is also heartwarming and bright, and they have the same endearing, easy-going laugh. Moreover, Blake's laugh has always reminded me of Alan Alda's beautiful laugh in the TV show, M*A*S*H.

Each spring, when we would drive past a hillside of blooming daffodils in Mariemont, I would tease Blake about how exciting it was that the earth was giggling in blooming flowers. He would then flash his beautiful smile, shake his head, and say, "Oh Muer." I'm often told that Blake looks just like his "top gun Grandfather Boyd."

Brooks's nickname was "Sweetie Baby," because he is the baby of the family, winning over everyone with a charismatic personality, huge heart, and a unique ability to inspire devotion from others. His love for animals is equally as endearing. Brooks views life and its challenges with an admirable can-do attitude coupled with an extraordinarily positive outlook. He exhibits the strong leadership trait of having a growth mindset just like the one we learned about in Building Block 6.

As a mom, my priority in raising you two boys was to plant three seeds and nurture those seeds so that they would take hold in perpetuity: 1) to accept Christ as your Savior and to reflect His love in all that you do, 2) to become best friends with your brother, which would secure a lifelong support system, and 3) to grow close to your Grandmom and provide her happiness into her sunset years. I am proud to say that all three seeds took root, grew, and blossomed. Moreover, your dad and I felt it was important to use our annual family vacations not only to enjoy fun, bonding time but also to expose you to the world's breathtaking beauty and profound history. We have such fond memories of traveling to the

US national parks and their surrounding city gems and traveling abroad. For example, our Wyoming dude ranch vacation was a family favorite. The time has come for you to embark on your own adventures, leading your future families into a world of exploration and discovery. We encourage you to carry on the Adams's tradition of traveling and seeing all you can see of God's amazing creation. Remember, if you don't learn at least one new thing each day, it's a dull day. Take heart in knowing we are incredibly proud of the both of you living joyful, successful lives . . . Blake with a happy marriage to Stephanie and Brooks enjoying a wonderful relationship with Morgan. My heart will always beat with unconditional love for you both.

My advice to you moving forward is to put Christ first in all things. When we were newlyweds, your dad and I would always say that we would begin our new life together building our marriage on the firm foundation of Christ, so when life's storms inevitably blow our way, our marriage and life would be protected. We started by finding a church to regularly worship and spending time together in a couple's devotional. In turn, He will reward your faithfulness with His faithfulness by taking care of your future families. Retain your childhood's effervescence, kindheartedness, and warmth. Keep a sense of humor throughout each day. It's a gift to be able to see the funny side of life, which allows us to not take things too seriously and encourages us to find the good. As I always say, if you look for the bad in others, you will find the bad. However, if you look for the good in others, you will find the good instead. Be the kind of person who discovers the good. Queen Elizabeth II wittily remarked, "Let us not take ourselves too seriously. None of us has a monopoly on wisdom." Enjoy yourself—stop and smell the roses. Time passes quickly, and it will startle you when the time is up. A good rule of thumb is not to wait until it's just the right time to do something important because the time will never be just right. Remember that we are forgiven when we forgive. There is valor in unity and moving forward. Last but not least, continue to make us proud by making Christ proud, being gentlemen to all, and, of course, being *polished.*

Love you forever,
Mom

Protocol School of Washington (PSOW)

Dear Pamela and PSOW team,

Please accept my sincerest gratitude for the certification, training, and alumni relations support you have provided over the years to my mom and me. It is an honor to share my credentials because the PSOW is the gold standard in our global community, having trained over four thousand corporate etiquette consultants in over sixty-eight countries. The PSOW has empowered its graduates for more than thirty years in business etiquette, business image consulting, communication, and international protocol training. I am proud to share that I am certified and trained by the only school of its kind that is nationally accredited and recognized by the US Department of Education, as well as being a certified women-owned business by the WBENC. I am equally proud that my company, Cincinnati Etiquette & Leadership Institute, is also WBE-certified. It was a reassurance to know that at any time during the writing process of *Polished,* I could reach out and gain intellectual support from the alumni relations department of PSOW. You truly offer an exceptional lifetime partnership to your students.

To be a second-generation PSOW graduate means the world to me since it was an honor to my mom that her daughter followed in her footsteps. The PSOW will always have my loyalty and dedication. Your teaching, delivery methods, and impeccable standards of doing business are extraordinary, and this benefits CELI's clients and *Polished* readers. Pamela, I remain grateful for your friendship because, as we agree, at the end of the day, the most important element in any business is meaningful relationship-building. You are my lifelong friend, both personally and professionally.

Highest regards,
Tiffany

GREENLEAF BOOK GROUP

Dear Greenleaf Book Group,

You deserve many accolades for all of your hard work helping *Polished* make its debut to the world. I am appreciative for my amazingly talented and dedicated teams and highly recommend Greenleaf's services to new and seasoned authors. You are consummate professionals who contributed expertise and enthusiasm throughout each stage of development and distribution. The publishing process for a new author could have gone one of two ways: either each stage could have felt like "death by a thousand paper cuts" or "smooth sailing all the way." I am happy to report partnering with Greenleaf was the latter, smooth sailing all the way! There were other major publishers who approached me about the prospect of publishing *Polished*. I was often asked, "Why Greenleaf?" From day one, the team was courteous, professional, conscientious, and brilliant. Initially, I recall being told by Greenleaf to prepare myself because less than 10% of all book submissions are accepted. When you shared the good news that *Polished* overwhelmingly made the cut and how excited you were to collaborate because of its "evergreen, boutique topic that is in high demand," I was moved beyond measure.

LETTERS OF ACKNOWLEDGMENT

Tone at the top matters. It became clear that I made the correct choice when the CEO of Greenleaf, Tanya Hall, emailed me to congratulate me and offered her personal contact information. She extended an earnest offer to call her directly should I ever have a question or concern. Tanya also mailed me her insightful book that she wrote to provide guidance to new authors. What dedication from the upper echelon to her authors. This dedication didn't stop at the C-suite level but also permeated throughout the company. During the manuscript development process, my ideas were heard and validated. I was impressed with each interaction and correspondence. I could share my opinion candidly, and you always figured out a way to guide me with your industry and reader knowledge, but also incorporate my personal style and unique voice.

A special thank you goes to Tanya Hall, Daniel Sandoval, Lindsey Clark, Lindsay Bohls, Kim Lance, Tiffany Barrientos, and Amanda Marquette. My heartfelt gratitude extends to my freelance editors. Many thanks goes to Claudia Volkman, Marianne Tatom, and Killian Piraro who were incredibly helpful and gifted with their craft. A special shout out goes to James Buchanan and Amanda Hughes who set the gold standard in editing and are pure literary geniuses. James provided patient support and a critical eye when I needed it the most. Amanda was brilliant in her wordsmithing and the way she puts together her nouns and verbs is magical and unmatched. I came a long way as a new author thanks to their patience and guidance. When the stars align again to possibly author my next book, I will definitely return to the doorstep of Greenleaf Book Group excitedly knocking. Thank you for your dedication in making this literary journey so personally fulfilling and fun!

Gratefully yours,
Tiffany

OLLIE

Dear Ollie,

Being a 75-pound Golden Retriever, you might need some help from a human to read this letter. Authoring a book is exciting and intellectually stimulating, but can also feel isolating, especially during a pandemic lockdown. You were my loyal furry companion who stayed by my side eager to comfort me and always in a good mood. Whether it was a wagging tail, sweet disposition, or goofball antics, you brought smiles to my face when I needed them the most. During my occasional writer's block, you would always be up for a walk to help clear the cobwebs from my head and faithfully meet me at the freezer for an ice cube handout. When you chew ice, you have an uncanny way of making each cube sound scrumptious. Thank you, "O," for your loving presence and faithful companionship. You're a good boy.

Hugs,
Mom

A Note of Gratitude from the Author

Dear Valued Reader,

Please accept my sincere gratitude for the privilege of your time and attention while embarking on this learning journey to be your polished best. I take your trust and support seriously. It's my goal that you depart from the pages of this book different from when you arrived. I have the utmost confidence that your investment of energy in reading this book will yield fruitful new beginnings for your career as your higher self emerges while employing these modern business etiquette strategies. Embrace the opportunity that lies before you as you harness this new mindset to yield results. Simply put, challenge yourself to be the change you want to be. I am a strong believer in the quotes used throughout this book. Quotes add rich value to our lives, so I will leave you with a final piece of advice from Winston Churchill: "Continuous effort—not strength or intelligence—is the key to unlocking our potential."

Best wishes for prosperity and excellence as you seek to find the coveted pearl of a new, emboldened you.

To excellence from all and for all with modern business etiquette!

Gratefully yours,
Tiffany L. Adams

About the Author

TIFFANY L. ADAMS, Founder and President of the Cincinnati Etiquette & Leadership Institute, LLC (CELI), is a certified Corporate Etiquette & International Protocol Expert as well as an accomplished instructor, consultant, public speaker, and published writer. Adams was born in Norman, Oklahoma, and was raised a proud "military brat," a moniker she wears with a badge of honor. Military children often develop a unique resilience due to multiple moves and varied cultural experiences. They also feel a deep sense of patriotism and have an exceptional respect for protocol. In addition to earning her BS in Finance at Miami University of Oxford, Ohio, and an MBA in Finance from the University of Cincinnati, she has more than fifteen years of work experience in the financial services industry and nonprofit sector. Adams proudly worked the longevity of her banking career at US Bancorp. It was at US Bancorp where she had the privilege of working for Richard Davis (formerly Chairman and CEO of US Bancorp) and was mentored by Mr. Davis thereafter. Adams has also been trained and certified by the Protocol School of Washington—the only school of its kind to be nationally accredited and recognized by the U.S. Department of Education.

At CELI, Adams's mission is to empower clients with an essential yet often overlooked professional development skill set: modern business etiquette. CELI's curriculum is enriched by courses from Harvard University as well as Babson College's Executive Women's Leadership Program. CELI is certified as a national Women's Business Enterprise (WBE), which promotes its clients' vendor diversity programs. Adams was featured in PNC Bank's "Women Who Achieve," celebrating women entrepreneurs and executives for their successful business endeavors. Adams was a member of the Business Leaders Alliance (BLA), which connects business leaders with aspiring college students. She served on ArtsWave's Campaign Leadership Cabinet and was co-chair of ArtsWave's Women's Leadership Roundtable. Her blog, *Ms. Tiffany's Epiphanies*®, can be found at www.etiquetteplease.com.

Adams and her husband and soulmate, Doug, reside in Cincinnati and have a golden retriever named Ollie. They have two sons: Blake, who works for Grainger and is happily married to Stephanie in Chicago, and Brooks, who is employed in sales at Procter & Gamble. Adams is the proud daughter of a U.S.A.F. colonel and fighter pilot who was awarded the highest honor in the Air Force, the Distinguished Flying Cross, for heroism in aerial flight and combat. Adams's mother was a dedicated teacher with her PhD in gifted education and inspired Adams's passion for etiquette by also graduating from the Protocol School of Washington and being her best friend in life. Adams's priorities in life are faith, family, and encouraging others to be the finest ambassadors of themselves that they can be so we all can leave this world a bit better than we found it.

Made in the USA
Las Vegas, NV
08 June 2024

90894997R00215